ELLE
KNITTING COLLECTION

ELLE®
KNITTING COLLECTION
50 Exclusive Designs from France

Translated and Edited by Sandy Carr

CRESSET PRESS
LONDON SYDNEY AUCKLAND JOHANNESBURG

This edition published in 1989 by Cresset Press, an imprint of
Century Hutchinson Ltd, Brookmount House, 62-65 Chandos Place,
Covent Garden, London WC2N 4NW

Century Hutchinson Australia Pty Limited, 89-91 Albion Street,
Surry Hills, Sydney, New South Wales 2010, Australia

Century Hutchinson New Zealand Limited, PO Box 40-086,
Glenfield, Auckland 10, New Zealand

Century Hutchinson South Africa Pty Limited, PO Box 337,
Bergvlei, 2012 South Africa

British Library Cataloguing in Publication Data
The Elle Knitting collection: 50 exclusive designs from France
   1. Knitting-France-Patterns
   2. Clothing and dress
   I. Carr, Sandy
   646.4'304   TT819.F7
   ISBN 0 7126 2410 4

Designed by Patrick McLeavey and Sue Storey
Additional text by Sandy Carr
Patterns checked by Marilyn Wilson
Additional photography by Simon Butcher
Additional illustrations by Lilly Whitlock

Yarns supplied courtesy of
Laine Couture, 20 Bedford Street, London WC2E 9HP
Colourspun, 18 Camden Road, London NW1
The Yarn Store Ltd, 8 Gaunton Street, London W1V 1LJ

International Textile Care Labelling Code courtesy
of the Home Laundering Consultative Council

Printed and bound in Singapore

Contents

Contents

Introduction

Knitting is an ancient craft that has recently taken on a new lease of life. The dreary patterns and drab yarns of some years ago have given way to a sudden flood of creative ideas and innovative designs. At the same time there has been an extraordinary wave of technical innovation in the matter of new yarns and knitting materials. Contemporary designers have made abundant use of these materials but they have also, on the whole, rejected much of the complex shaping and intricacy of traditional knitting design in favour of bold shapes, interesting colour patterns and simple stitches. So knitting has become more exciting but also easier and less daunting for beginners in the craft.

Elle magazine, which has been essential monthly reading for thousands of French women for many years has, as one would expect, been in the forefront of this revolution in knitting habits. The French, in any case, have a long tradition of combining style and simplicity in knitting as in other domestic crafts and the patterns in this book, all first published in *Elle*, have that casual understated elegance that is the hallmark of French fashion generally.

There are fifty patterns in the following pages, ranging from very simple styles suitable for beginners to garments with more complicated stitch patterns or shaping, which will provide something more challenging for experienced knitters. All the patterns, which include men's and children's wear as well as women's garments, are rated according to their degree of difficulty with one, two or three stars. In addition, they are divided into seasonal groupings, although these should not be taken as hard and fast categories. For example, a 'summer' style made in cotton could be a highly suitable winter garment if made in a woollen yarn.

The patterns have been translated and entirely rewritten for English knitters. On page 119, however, American knitters will find some notes on terminology and metric/imperial measurements conversion charts which will enable them to follow the patterns quite easily. The abbreviations used in the patterns are explained below. In some cases there may be special abbreviations that are relevant to one particular pattern only and these are given on the same page as the pattern itself.

The yarns used in the original patterns were all French and many of them are unobtainable, or obtainable only in a few specialist shops, in this country. For those who are able to find them, a list of these yarns is given on page 126 but otherwise the yarns quoted in the patterns are described in general terms only as 'double knitting', 'four ply', and so on. While this does allow you to choose among the huge range of wonderful yarns on the market, it also means that the choice must be exercised with more than the usual caution. Advice on choosing and buying yarn for these patterns is given on page 116. It is essential to read this very carefully before making a purchase. Before beginning work on any pattern it is also advisable to consult the section beginning on page 118, where guidance on following the patterns and, in particular, on reading colour and stitch pattern charts will be found. Where, as here, the yarns quoted are not branded ones, it is doubly important to make scrupulous tension checks. Do not embark on any pattern until you are absolutely sure that you have matched your tension to that specified in the pattern. Information on measuring and checking tension is given on page 120.

Abbreviations

alt – alternate(ly)
approx – approximately
beg – begin(ning)
cm – centimetre(s)
cont – continu(e)(ing)
dec – decreas(e)(es)(ing)
foll – follow(s)(ing)
g – gram(s)
g st – garter stitch (see page 121)
inc – increas(e)(es)(ing)
K – knit
K up – pick up and knit
K-wise – knitwise, as if to knit
LH – left-hand
mm – millimetres
P – purl
patt – pattern
psso – pass slipped stitch over

p2sso – pass 2 slipped stitches over
P up – pick up and purl
P-wise – purlwise, as if to purl
rem – remain(s)(ing)
rep – repeat(s)
RH – right-hand
RS – right side
sl – slip
st(s) – stitch(es)
st st – stocking stitch (see page 121)
tbl – through the back of the loop (s)
tog – together
WS – wrong side
ybk – yarn between the needles to back of work
yfwd – yarn forward
yon – yarn over needle
yrn – yarn round needle

STAR RATINGS

Easy to make, suitable for beginners

More difficult, for knitters with some experience

Challenging, requires expert skills for a perfect finish

Pretty Pink

Moss stitch worked in fine soft cotton makes the perfect fabric for a casual straight-sleeved sweater with a deep waist rib.

SIZES
To fit (81)86(91)cm bust

MATERIALS
(450)450(500)g four-ply yarn
1 pair each 2¼mm and 3¼mm needles

TENSION
22 sts and 40 rows to 10cm over moss st on 3¼mm needles.

FRONT
Using 2¼mm needles, cast on (104)110(116) sts.
Work 14cm K2, P2 rib.**
Change to 3¼mm needles.
Cont in moss st until work measures (25)26(27)cm from top of rib, ending with a WS row.
Divide for neck
Next row Patt (52)55(58) sts, turn, leaving rem sts on a spare needle, cont on these sts only for left side of neck.
***Next row** Work 2 tog, patt to end. (51)54(57) sts.
Next row Patt to end.
Rep last 2 rows twice more then first row again. Patt 3 rows.
Next row Work 2 tog, patt to end. Patt 1 row.****
Rep from *** to **** 4 times more. Now dec 1 st at neck edge on next and foll 2 alt rows. (24)27(30) sts.
Work 0[4:8] rows straight.
Shape shoulder
Cast off (8)9(10) sts at beg of next and foll alt row. (8)9(10) sts.
Work 1 row.
Cast off.

Return to sts on spare needle, with RS of work facing rejoin yarn to centre st. Complete to match left side of neck, working from *** to end, and working 1 more row before shoulder shaping.

BACK
Work as given for front to **
Change to 3¼mm needles.
Cont in moss st until work measures same as front to beg of shoulder shaping.
Shape shoulders
Cast off (8)9(10) sts at beg of next 6 rows. 56 sts.
Cast off.

SLEEVES
Using 2¼mm needles, cast on (94)100(106) sts.
Work 14cm K2, P2 rib.
Change to 3¼mm needles and work in moss st until sleeve measures (39)40(41)cm from top of rib.
Cast off.

NECKBAND
Using 2¼mm needles, cast on 150 sts.
Work in K2, P2 rib, inc 1 st at each end of every alt row until there are 166 sts. Work 1 row, leave these sts on a length of yarn.

MAKING UP
Join shoulder seams. Set in sleeves flat, matching centre of cast-off edge to shoulder seam. Join shaped edges of neckband. Join on neckband beg at centre front with neckband seam and sew through each st in turn to neck edge. Join side and sleeve seams.

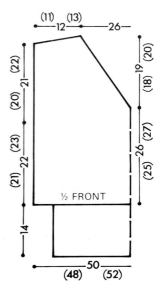

½ FRONT

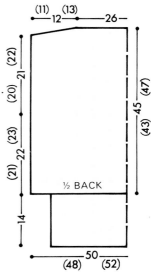

½ BACK

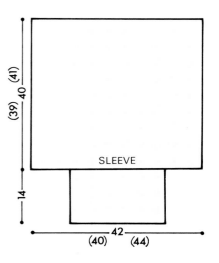

SLEEVE

Photograph: A. Carrara   Designed by Ginou Comiti for Véra Finbert

Flower Border

**A pretty flower-decked cardigan
worked in fine four-ply yarn.**

SPRING
★ ★ ★

SIZES
To fit (81)86(91)cm bust

MATERIALS
(450)450(500)g four-ply yarn in main
colour(A)
50g in each of 9 contrast colours (B, C, D,
E, F, G, H, J, L)
1 pair each 2¼mm and 3mm needles
7 buttons

TENSION
28 sts and 34 rows to 10cm over patt on
3mm needles.

RIGHT FRONT
Using 2¼mm needles and A, cast on
(61)64(67) sts. Work 7cm K1, P1 rib.
Change to 3mm needles and work 4 rows
st st. Commence patt from chart 1:
1st row (RS) *K1B, 1A, 1B, 3A, 1B, 1A,
  1B, 3A; rep from * to last (1)4(7) sts,
  (1B) 1B, 1A, 1B, 1A (1B, 1A, 1B, 3A, 1B).
2nd row P(1A)2A, 1B, 1A(3B, 2A, 1B,
  1A), *[1A, 3B] twice, 2A, 1B, 1A; rep
  from * to end.
These 2 rows establish the position of
chart 1. Cont in patt working from chart 1.
When all 52 rows of chart 1 have been
completed, work 11 rows st st in A.
Commence patt from chart 2:
1st row (WS) P(1A) 0(3A), *1J, 3A; rep
  from * to end.
2nd row K to end in A.
3rd row P(1A) 0(3A), *1H, 3A; rep from *
  to end.
4th row *K2A, 3H, 3A; rep from * to last
  (5)0(3) sts, (2A, 3H)0(2A, 1H).
These 4 rows establish the position of
chart 2. Cont in patt from chart 2 until all
9 rows are completed.
Cont in st st and A until work measures
(29)30(31)cm from top of rib, ending with
a RS row.
Shape armhole
Cast off 6 sts at beg of next row, then 3 sts
at beg of foll 2 alt rows, now dec 1 st at
armhole edge on next and every foll alt
row until (45)48(51) sts rem.
Work straight until front measures
(35)37(39)cm, ending with a WS row.
Commence patt from chart 3:
1st row (RS) *K2A, 1C, 3A, 1C, 1A; rep
  from * to last (5)0(3) sts, (2A, 1C,
  2A)0(2A, 1C).
2nd row P(1A, 3C, 1A)0(2C, 1A), *4A, 3C,
  1A; rep from * to end.
These 2 rows establish the position of
chart 3. Cont in patt from chart 3 until
work measures (39)41(43)cm from top of
rib, ending with a WS row.
Shape neck
Keeping chart 3 correct, cast off 12 sts at
beg of next row, then 2 sts at beg of foll 3
alt rows. (27)30(33) sts.

Now dec 1 st at neck edge on 3 foll 4th
rows (when chart 3 is completed, work in
st st in A) then work straight until
armhole measures (17)18(19)cm, ending
at armhole edge.
Shape shoulder
Cast off (8)9(10) sts at beg of next and foll
alt row. Work 1 row.
Cast off rem (8)9(10) sts.

LEFT FRONT
Work as given for right front, reversing
patts from charts 1, 2 and 3 and all
shapings.

BACK
Using 2¼mm needles and A, cast on
(123)129(135) sts. Work 7cm K1, P1 rib.
Change to 3mm needles and work 4 rows
st st. Commence patt from chart 1:
1st row (RS) K(1B)3A, 1B(1B), *1A, 1B,
  3A, 1B, 1A, 1B, 3A, 1B; rep from * to
  last (2)5(2) sts, (1A, 1B)1A, 1B, 3A(1A,
  1B).
2nd row P(1A, 1B)2B, 2A, 1B(1A, 1B),
  *2A, 3B, 1A, 3B, 2A, 1B; rep from * to
  last (1)4(1) sts, (1A)2A, 2B(1A).
These 2 rows establish the position of
chart 1. When chart 1 is completed work

Chart 1

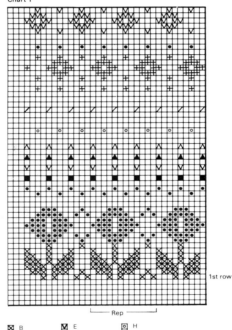

Chart 2

Chart 3

Chart 4

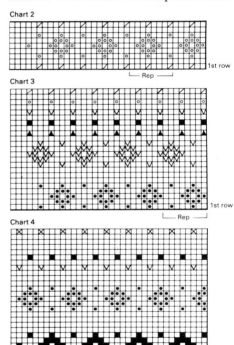

1st row

Rep

⊠	B		⋎	E		⊡	H
⊡	C		▲	F		⊟	J
■	D		⊠	G		⊞	L

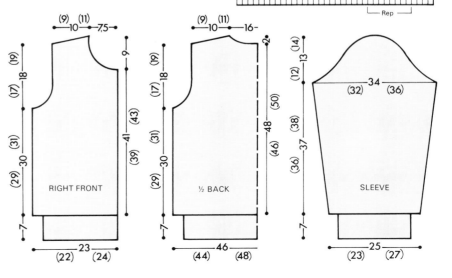

| | RIGHT FRONT | | ½ BACK | | SLEEVE |

Photograph: M. Yavel   Designed by Odile Cherer for Fac Bazaar

11 rows st st in A.
Now work 9 rows from chart 2.
Cont in st st and A until work measures (29)30(31)cm from top of rib.

Shape armholes
Cast off 6 sts at beg of next 2 rows, then 3 sts at beg of foll 4 rows, now dec 1 st at each end of next and 3 foll alt rows. (91)97(103) sts.
 Work straight until back measures (35)37(39)cm, ending with a WS row.
Now work patt from chart 3 until back measures 4 rows less than left front at shoulder, ending with a WS row.

Divide for neck
Next row Patt (34)37(40) sts, turn, leaving rem sts on a spare needle, cont on these sts only for right side of neck.
Cont in patt from chart 3 (work in st st in A only when chart 3 is completed), cast off 5 sts at beg of next and foll alt row.

Shape shoulder
Cast off (8)9(10) sts at beg of next and foll alt row. Work 1 row. Cast off.
Return to sts on spare needle, with RS of work facing rejoin yarn to next st, cast off 23 sts, patt to end. (34)37(40) sts. Work 1 row. Complete to match right side of neck.

SLEEVES
Using 2¼mm needles and A, cast on (63)69(75) sts. Work 7cm K1, P1 rib.
Change to 3mm needles and work 4 rows st st in A. Commence patt from chart 4:
1st row (RS) K(3A)2A(1A), *1J, 3A; rep from * to last (0)3(2) sts, (0)1J, 2A(1J, 1A).
This row establishes the position of chart 4. Cont in patt from chart 4 inc 1 st at each end of 13 foll 8th rows. (85)95(101) sts.
When chart 4 is completed, cont to inc as set, work 5 rows st st in A, then work patt from chart 1, work 11 rows st st in A, work patt from chart 2.
Cont in st st in A only until sleeve measures (36)37(38)cm from top of rib.

Shape top
Cast off 4 sts at beg of next 2 rows, then 3 sts at beg of foll 2 rows, then 2 sts at beg of foll 4 rows. Now dec 1 st, then 2 sts alternately, on each end of every alt row (6)7(8) times. 31 sts.
Now cast off 2 sts at beg of next 2 rows, then 3 sts at beg of foll 4 rows. Cast off.

NECKBAND
Using 2¼mm needles and A, cast on 9 sts. Work in K1, P1 rib until band when slightly stretched fits round neck edge. Cast off in rib.

RIGHT FRONT BAND
Using 2¼mm needles and A, cast on 8 sts. Work 2 cm K1, P1 rib. Make buttonhole:
1st buttonhole row Rib 3, cast off 2 sts, rib to end.
2nd buttonhole row Rib to end, cast on 2 sts over those cast off in previous row.
Cont in rib until band fits up right front edge, making 6 more buttonholes at (7)7.5(8)cm intervals. Cast off in rib.

LEFT FRONT BAND
Work as given for right front band omitting buttonholes.

MAKING UP
Join shoulder seams. Join side and sleeve seams. Set in sleeves. Join on neck and front bands. Sew on buttons.

Ribbed Tweed

Tweedy fabrics can be simulated using special flecked yarns or by working several coloured yarns together. This easy-going sweater could also be made in a plain wool or cotton.

SIZES
To fit (81)86(91)cm bust

MATERIALS
(550)600(650)g double knitting yarn
1 pair each 3mm and 4mm needles
1 set four double-pointed 3mm needles

TENSION
29 sts and 32 rows to 10cm over patt on 4mm needles.

FRONT
Using 3mm needles, cast on (119)125(131) sts.
Work 3cm K1, P1 rib, inc 8 sts evenly over last row. (127)133(139) sts.
Change to 4mm needles.
Commence patt:
1st row (RS) K(1)0(1), *K2, P1, K1; rep from * to last (2)1(2) sts, K(2)1(2).
2nd row K(1)0(1), P1, *K3, P1; rep from * to last (1)0(1) sts, K(1)0(1).
These 2 rows form the patt rep.
Cont in patt until work measures (35)36(37)cm from top of rib, ending with a WS row.
Shape armholes
Cast off 5 sts at beg of next 2 rows, then 4 sts at beg of foll 2 rows. Now dec 2 sts at each end of next and foll alt row, and 1 st at each end of foll 2 alt rows. (97)103(109)sts.**
Now work straight until front measures (49)51(53)cm from top of rib, ending with a WS row.
Divide for neck
Next row Patt (40)43(46) sts, turn, leaving rem sts on a spare needle, cont on these sts only for left side of neck.
Shape neck
***Cast off 4 sts at neck edge on next row, 3 sts on foll alt row, 2 sts on next alt row, then 1 st on foll alt row. (30)33(36) sts.
Now work straight until armhole measures (20)21(22)cm from beg, ending at armhole edge.
Shape shoulder
Cast off (10)11(12) sts at beg of next and foll alt row. Work 1 row.
Cast off.
Return to sts on spare needle, with RS of work facing, rejoin yarn to next st.
Next row Cast off 17 sts, patt to end. (40)43(46) sts.
Work 1 row.
Now complete to match left side of neck from *** to end.

BACK
Work as given for front to **.
Now work straight until back measures 4 rows less than front to shoulder, ending with a WS row.

Divide for neck
Next row Patt (42)45(48) sts, turn, leaving rem sts on a spare needle, cont on these sts only for right side of neck.
Shape neck
****Cast off 6 sts at neck edge on next and foll alt row. (30)33(36) sts.
Work straight until armhole measures (20)21(22)cm, ending at armhole edge.
Shape shoulder
Cast off (10)11(12) sts at beg of next and foll alt row. (10)11(12) sts.
Work 1 row.
Cast off.
Return to sts on spare needle, with RS of work facing, rejoin yarn to next st.
Next row Cast off 13 sts, patt to end. (42)45(48) sts.
Work 1 row.
Complete to match right side of neck, working from **** to end.

SLEEVES
Using 3mm needles, cast on (67)73(79) sts.
Work 3cm K1, P1 rib.
Change to 4mm needles and work in patt as given for front, inc 1 st at each end of every 10th row until there are (89)95(101) sts.
Now work straight until sleeve measures (45)46(47)cm from top of rib, ending with a WS row.
Shape top
Cast off (5)6(7) sts at beg of next 2 rows, then 2 sts at beg of foll 4 rows. Now dec 1 st at each end of next and every alt row until there are (33)35(37) sts.
Now cast off 3 sts at beg of foll 4 rows. (21)23(25) sts. Cast off.

MAKING UP
Join shoulder seams. Join side and sleeve seams. Set in sleeves.
Neckband
Using double-pointed 3mm needles, K up 116 sts round neck edge.
Work 3cm K1, P1 rib in rounds.
Cast off loosely in rib.

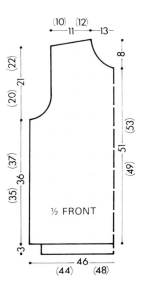

½ FRONT

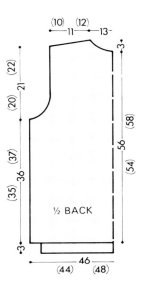

½ BACK

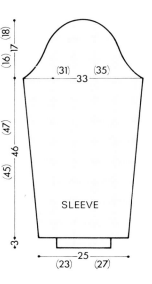

SLEEVE

Photograph: Grignaschi   Designed by Françoise Gilbert

Scottie

A pair of lovable puppy motifs are featured on a child's cardigan. The pattern is given for a plain back but the motifs could easily be worked on that too.

SIZES
To fit age (4)6(8) years

MATERIALS
(100)150(200)g four-ply yarn in main colour (A)
100g in 1st contrast colour (B)
50g in 2nd contrast colour (C)
1 pair each 2¼mm and 3mm needles
5 buttons

TENSION
25 sts and 28 rows to 10cm over st st on 3mm needles.

RIGHT FRONT
Using 2¼mm needles and A, cast on (41)43(45) sts. Work 5cm K1, P1 rib.
Change to 3mm needles and commence patt from chart 1:
1st row (RS) With A, K to end.
2nd row P(1C)2A, 1C(1B, 3A, 1C), *3A, 3B, 3A, 1C; rep from * to end.
3rd row *K1B, 4A; rep from * to last (1)3(5) sts, (1B)1B, 2A(1B, 4A).
4th row P(1B)1A, 2B(3A, 2B), *1B, 7A, 2B; rep from * to end.
These 4 rows set the position of chart 1.
Cont in st st working colour patt from chart 1 until all 7 rows of chart are completed.
Work (15)19(23) rows st st in B.
Commence motif from chart 2:
1st row (RS) K(10)11(12)B, 6A, 4B, 11A, (10)11(12)B.
2nd row P all the A sts in A and all the B sts in B.

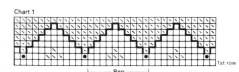

Chart 1

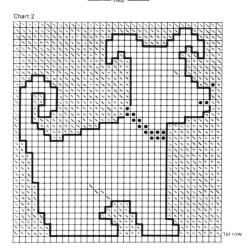

Chart 2

3rd row K (11)12(13)B, 6A, 4B, 11A, (9)10(11)B.
4th row P(9)10(11)B, 9A, 6B, 5A, (12)13(14)B.
These 4 rows set the position of the motif on chart 2.
Cont in st st working motif from chart 2 as set until right front measures (17)20(23) cm from top of rib, ending with a WS row.
Shape neck and armhole
Keep chart correct then cont in B only, dec 1 st at beg of next and foll 16 alt rows, *at the same time*, when work measures (18)20(22)cm from top of rib, cast off 6 sts at LH edge for armhole.
Cont to dec as set at neck edge until armhole measures (9)10(11)cm, ending with a WS row.
Now work 6 rows colour patt from chart 3.
Cont in st st in A until armhole measures (13)14(15)cm.
Cast off.

Chart 3

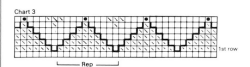

Rep

LEFT FRONT
Work as given for right front reversing motif from chart 2 thus:
1st row (RS) K(10)11(12)B, 11A, 4B, 6A, (10)11(12)B.
2nd row P all the A sts in A and all the B sts in B.
3rd row K (9)10(11)B, 11A, 4B, 6A, (11)12(13)B.
4th row P(12)13(14)B, 5A, 6B, 9A, (9)10(11)B.
These 4 rows set the position of the reversed motif.
Complete left front to match right front reversing all shapings.

BACK
Using 2¼mm needles and A, cast on (74)78(82) sts.
Work 5cm K1, P1 rib.
Change to 3mm needles and cont in st st until work measures (18)20(22)cm from top of rib.
Shape armholes
Cast off 6 sts at beg of next 2 rows. (62)66(70) sts.
Cont in st st until armholes measure (13)14(15)cm from beg.
Shape shoulders
Cast off (18)20(22) sts at beg of next 2 rows. 26 sts.
Change to 2¼mm needles.
Work 6 rows K1, P1 rib.
Cast off in rib.

SLEEVES
Using 2¼mm needles and A, cast on (39)43(47) sts.
Work 4cm K1, P1 rib.
Change to 3mm needles and cont in st st, inc 1 st at each end of every foll (8th)9th(10th) row until there are (53)57(61) sts.
Work straight until sleeve measures (25)27(29)cm from top of rib.
Shape top
Cast off 2 sts at the beg of every foll row until 5 sts rem.
Cast off.

MAKING UP
Join shoulder seams.
Right front border
Using 2¼mm needles and A, with RS of work facing, K up (66)74(82) sts along right front opening to beg of neck shaping and 47 sts to shoulder. (113)121(129) sts.
Work 2 rows K1, P1 rib.
Make buttonholes:
Next row Rib 49, [work 2 tog, yfwd, rib (13)15(17)] 4 times, work 2 tog, yfwd, rib 2.
Rib 4 more rows.
Cast off in rib.
Left front border
Work to match right front border omitting buttonholes.
Join front border and neckband seams.
Join side and sleeve seams.
Set in sleeves.
Sew on buttons.

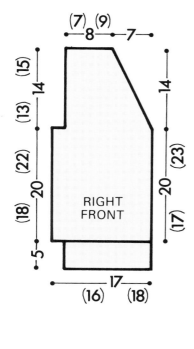

RIGHT FRONT

(7) (9)
8 — 7
(15) 14
(13)
(22) 20
(18)
5
17
(16) (18)
14
(23) 20
(17)

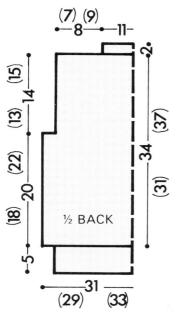

½ BACK

(7) (9)
8 — 11
(15) 14
(13)
(22) 20
(18)
5
31
(29) (33)
2
34 (37)
(31)

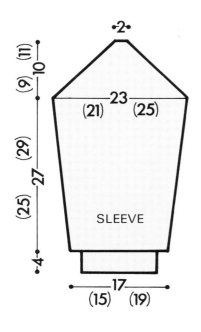

SLEEVE

2
(11) 10
(9)
23
(21) (25)
(29) 27
(25)
4
17
(15) (19)

Open-Necked Sweater

A wide set-in panel worked in stocking stitch on each side of the neck opening is the distinguishing feature of an otherwise simple seed stitch sweater.

SIZES
To fit (81)86(91)cm bust

MATERIALS
(700)750(800)g chunky yarn
1 pair each 6mm and 7mm needles
3 buttons

TENSION
12 sts and 19 rows to 10cm over patt on 7mm needles.

FRONT
Using 6mm needles, cast on (48)50(52) sts.
Work 9cm K1, P1 rib, inc 12 sts evenly across last row. (60)62(64) sts.
Change to 7mm needles and commence patt:
1st row (RS) K to end.
2nd row [P1, K1] to end.
3rd row K to end.
4th row [K1, P1] to end.
These 4 rows form the patt rep.
Cont in patt until work measures (36)37(38)cm from top of rib, ending with a WS row.
Divide for neck
Next row Patt (27)28(29) sts, turn, leaving rem sts on a spare needle, cont on these sts only for left side of neck.
**Next row P2, work 2 tog, patt to end.
Next row Patt to last 2 sts, K2.
Next row P2, patt to end.
Next row Patt to last 2 sts, K2.**
Rep from ** to ** once more, then the first row again. (24)25(26) sts.
Shape armhole
Next row Cast off 5 sts, patt to last 2 sts, K2. (19)20(21) sts.
Next row P2, patt to end.
Next row Patt to last 2 sts, K2.
Rep from ** to ** twice more. (17)18(19) sts. Work straight until armhole measures (17)18(19)cm. Cast off.
Return to sts on spare needle, with RS facing, rejoin yarn to next st, cast off 6 sts, patt to end. (27)28(29) sts.
Complete to match left side reversing shapings and st st border.

BACK
Using 6mm needles, cast on (48)50(52) sts.
Work 9cm K1, P1 rib, inc 12 sts evenly across last row. (60)62(64) sts.
Change to 7mm needles.
Cont in patt as given for front until back matches front to armhole shaping.
Shape armholes
Cast off 5 sts at beg of next 2 rows. (50)52(54) sts. Now work straight until armhole measures (17)18(19)cm.
Shape shoulders
Cast off (17)18(19) sts at beg of next 2 rows. Leave rem 16 sts on a st holder.

SLEEVES
Using 6mm needles, cast on (22)24(26) sts. Work 9cm K1, P1 rib, inc 10 sts evenly across last row. (32)34(36) sts.
Change to 7mm needles and cont in patt as given for front, inc 1 st at each end of every 14th row until there are (42)44(46) sts. Now work straight until sleeve measures (42)44(46)cm from top of rib. Cast off.

RIGHT FRONT NECKBAND
Using 7mm needles, with RS of work facing K up (23)24(25) sts along shaped edge of right front neck.
Next row P(13)14(15), turn.
Next row K to end.
Next row P(15)16(17), turn.
Next row K to end.
*** Cont in this way working 2 more sts from LH needle on each alt row until all sts are worked off, *at the same time* shape neck edge: cast off 4 sts at beg of next row, then dec 1 st at beg of foll 3 alt rows. (16)17(18) sts.
Now work straight until neckband measures 9cm at its widest point.
Cast off.

LEFT FRONT NECKBAND
Using 7mm needles, with WS of work facing P up (23)24(25) sts along shaped edge of left front neck.
Next row K(13)14(15), turn.
Next row P to end.
Next row K(15)16(17), turn.
Next row P to end.
Cont as given for right front neckband from *** until neckband measures approx 8cm at its widest point, ending with a P row.
Buttonhole row K2, [yfwd, K2 tog, K4] twice, yfwd, K2 tog, K(0)1(2).
Next row P to end.
Work straight until neckband measures 9cm at its widest point.
Cast off.

MAKING UP
Join shoulder seams.
Set in sleeves flat matching centre of cast-off edge to shoulder seam and joining last 4cm on each side to cast-off sts at underarm.
Sew front neckbands to front neck overlapping left side over right side.
Neckband
Using 6mm needles, with RS of work facing, K up 22 sts along top edge of right front neckband, K 16 sts from back neck st holder, now K up 22 sts along top edge of left front neckband. 60 sts.
Work in K1, P1 rib, inc 1 st at centre back neck on 1st row, and dec 1 st at each end of every alt row until there are 51 sts.
Now work straight until neckband measures 5cm. Cast off in rib.
Join side and sleeve seams.
Sew on buttons.

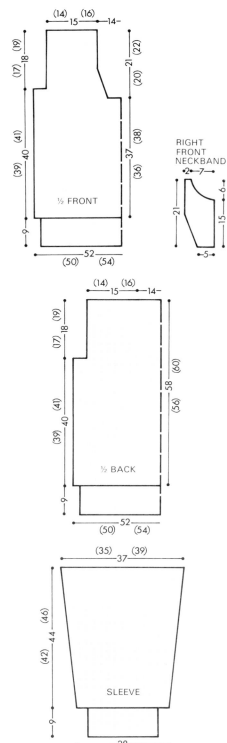

Photograph: J-C. Benoit Designed by Louise Beker for Pluck

Provençal

Pretty flower borders on a simple button-up cardigan. Make it in Shetland 2-ply jumper-weight wool or in fine cotton.

SIZES
To fit (81)86(91)cm bust

MATERIALS
(500)550(600)g four-ply yarn in main colour (A)
100g in 1st contrast colour (B)
50g in each of 5 contrast colours (C, D, E, F, G)
1 pair each 2¾mm and 3¼mm needles
7 buttons

TENSION
28 sts and 34 rows to 10cm over st st on 3¼mm needles.

RIGHT FRONT
Using 2¾mm needles and A, cast on (61)64(67) sts.
Work 4cm K1, P1 rib.
Change to 3¼mm needles and work 4 rows st st.
Commence patt from chart 1:
1st row (RS) K(1A)0(1A), *1C, 3A; rep from * to last (0)0(2) sts, (0)0(1C, 1A).
2nd row P(0)0(2A), *1A, 1D, 2A; rep from * to last (1)0(1) sts, (1A) 0(1A).
These 2 rows establish the position of chart 1. Cont working from chart 1 until all 12 rows have been completed.
Cont in st st and A until front measures (31)32(33)cm from top of rib, ending with a WS row.
Commence patt from chart 2:
1st row (RS) *K3A, 1B; rep from * to last (1)0(3) sts, (1A)0(3A).
2nd row P(1A)0(1A, 1B, 1A), *2A, 1B, 1A; rep from * to end.
These 2 rows establish the position of chart 2. Cont working from chart 2 until work measures (34)35(36)cm from top of rib, ending with a RS row.
Shape armhole
Cast off 5 sts at beg of next row, 3 sts at beg of foll alt row and 2 sts at beg of next alt row. Now dec 1 st at each end of next and foll 2 alt rows. (48)51(54) sts.
Cont in patt from chart 2 (when chart 2 is completed work in patt from chart 3) until front measures (45)47(49)cm from top of rib, ending with a WS row.
Shape neck
Cast off 12 sts at beg of next row, then 2 sts at beg of foll 3 alt rows. Now dec

1 st at neck edge on 3 foll 4th rows. (27)30(33) sts.
Work straight until armhole measures (20)21(22)cm, from beg, ending with a RS row.
Shape shoulder
Cast off (9)10(11) sts at beg of next and foll alt row.
Cast off rem (9)10(11) sts.

LEFT FRONT
Work as given for right front, reversing chart patts and all shapings.

BACK
Using 2¾mm needles and A, cast on (123)129(135) sts.
Work 4cm K1, P1 rib.
Change to 3¼mm needles and work 4 rows st st. Now work as given for right front working charts 1 and 2 as given for (3rd)1st(3rd) sizes of right front until back measures (34)35(36)cm from top of rib, ending on same patt row as right front to armhole.
Shape armholes
Cast off 5 sts at beg of next 2 rows, 3 sts at beg of foll 2 rows and 2 sts at beg of foll 2 rows. Now dec 1 st at each end of next and foll 2 alt rows. (97)103(109) sts.
Cont in patt from chart 2 (when chart 2 is completed) work in patt from chart 3) until back measures 4 rows less than front to shoulder, ending with a WS row.
Divide for neck
Next row Patt (37)40(43) sts, turn, leaving rem sts on a spare needle, cont on these sts only for right side of neck.
Cast off 5 sts at beg of next and foll alt row. (27)30(33) sts.
Shape shoulder
Cast off (9)10(11) sts at beg of next and foll alt row. Work 1 row.
Cast off.

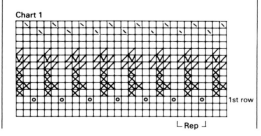

Chart 1

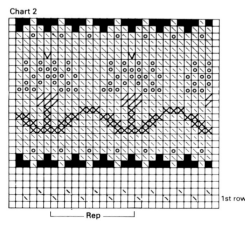

Chart 2

Return to sts on spare needle, with RS of work facing, rejoin yarn to next st, cast off 23 sts, patt to end. (37)40(43) sts.
Patt 1 row.
Complete to match right side of neck.

SLEEVES
Using 2¾mm needles and A, cast on (63)69(75) sts.
Work 4cm K1, P1 rib.
Change to 3¼mm needles and work 4 rows st st.
Cont in patt from chart 1 as given for (3rd)1st(3rd) sizes of right front, inc 1 st at each end of every foll 8th row until there are (89)95(101) sts (when chart 1 is complete cont in st st in A only).
Work straight until sleeve measures (34)35(36)cm from top of rib, ending with a WS row.
Now cont in patt from chart 2 as given for (1st)3rd(1st) sizes of right front, until sleeve measures approx (37)38(39)cm from top of rib, ending on same patt row as right front to armhole.
Shape top
Cont in patt from chart 2 (and chart 3 when chart 2 is completed), cast off 3 sts at beg of next 4 rows, then 2 sts at beg of foll 4 rows. Now dec 1 st at each end of every alt row until (35)37(39) sts rem. Now cast off 2 sts at beg of next 4 rows and 3 sts at beg of foll 2 rows. Dec 1 st at each end of every alt row until (15)17(19) sts rem.
Cast off.

NECKBAND
Using 2¾mm needles and A, cast on 9 sts.
Work in K1, P1 rib until band when slightly stretched fits neck edge.
Cast off.

RIGHT FRONT BAND
Using 2¾mm needles and A, cast on 8 sts.
Work 2cm K1, P1 rib.
Make buttonhole:
1st buttonhole row Rib 3, cast off 2 sts, rib to end.
2nd buttonhole row Rib to end, casting on 2 sts over those cast off in previous row.
Cont in rib, making 6 more buttonholes at (8)8(8.5)cm intervals, until band measures (51)53(55)cm from beg.
Cast off in rib.

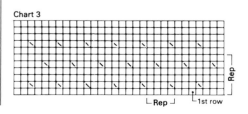

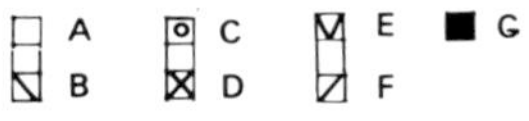

Chart 3

Photograph: J.-B. Maudin   Designed by Mireille Arouh for Fac Bazaar

LEFT FRONT BAND
Work as given for right front band omitting buttonholes.

MAKING UP
Join side and shoulder seams.
Join sleeve seams and set in sleeves matching jacquard bands.
Join on neck border. Join on right and left front borders. Sew on buttons.

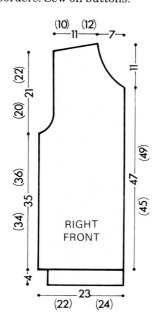

RIGHT FRONT

(10) (12)
11 — 7
(22)
21 20
(20)
(36)
35 (34)
(49)
47 (45)
•4
23
(22) (24)

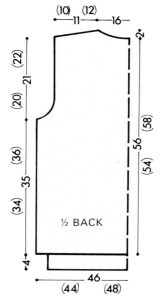

½ BACK

(10) (12)
11 — 16
2
(22)
21
(20)
56 (58)
(54)
(36)
35 (34)
•4
46
(44) (48)

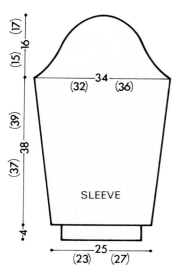

SLEEVE

(17)
16 (15)
34
(32) (36)
(39)
38 (37)
•4
25
(23) (27)

19

Colourslip Raglan

**A two-colour slipstitch pattern is
used for a classic raglan sweater
knitted in fine wool.**

SPRING
★ ★

SIZES
To fit (96)101(106)cm chest

MATERIALS
(400)450(500)g four-ply yarn in main
colour (A)
(250)300(350)g in contrast colour (B)
1 pair each 2¾mm and 3¼mm needles
1 set four double-pointed 2¾mm needles

TENSION
29 sts and 46 rows to 10cm over patt on
3¼mm needles.

FRONT
Using 2¾mm needles and A, cast on
(123)129(135) sts.
Work 8cm K1, P1 rib, inc 32 sts evenly
across last row. (155)161(167) sts.
Change to 3¼mm needles and commence
patt:
1st row (RS) With A, K to end.
2nd row As 1st row.
3rd row With B, [K1, sl 1 P-wise] to last
    st, K1.
4th row With B, [P1, sl 1 P-wise] to last
    st, P1.
These 4 rows form patt rep.
Cont in patt until work measures
(34)35(36)cm from top of rib, ending with
a RS row.**
Shape raglans
Cast off (2)3(4) sts at beg of next 2 rows,
then dec 1 st at each end of every alt row
until 73 sts rem, ending with a WS row.
Divide for neck
Next row Work 2 tog, patt 24 sts, turn,
    leaving rem sts on a spare needle, cont
    on these sts only for left side neck.
    25 sts.
Cont to dec for raglan on every alt row as
set, *at the same time* cast off 3 sts at neck
edge on next row and 2 sts at neck edge on
foll alt row, then dec 1 st at neck edge on
foll 9 alt rows.
Fasten off.
Return to sts on spare needle, with RS of
work facing, rejoin yarn to next st, cast off
21 sts, patt to last 2 sts, work 2 tog. 25 sts.
Work 1 row.
Complete to match left side of neck
reversing all shaping.

BACK
Work as given for front to **.
Shape raglans
Cast off (2)3(4) sts at beg of next 2 rows.
(151)155(159) sts.
Now dec 1 st at each end of every foll alt
row until 39 sts rem.
Cast off.

LEFT SLEEVE
Using 2¾mm needles and A, cast on
(67)73(79) sts.

Work 8cm K1, P1 rib, inc 28 sts evenly
across last row. (95)101(107) sts.
Change to 3¼mm needles and cont in patt
as given for front, inc 1 st at each end of
every foll 10th row until there are
(123)129(135) sts.
Work straight until sleeve measures
(37)38(39)cm from top of rib, ending with
a RS row.
Shape raglans
Cast off (2)3(4) sts at beg of next 2 rows.
Now dec 1 st at each end of every foll alt
row until 17 sts rem, ending with a RS
row.***
Now cast off 3 sts at beg of next and foll alt
row, then 2 sts at beg of foll 3 alt rows, *at
the same time* cont to dec 1 st on RH edge
as set at beg of foll 5 alt rows.
Fasten off.

RIGHT SLEEVE
Work as given for left sleeve to ***.
Complete to match left sleeve reversing
shaping.

MAKING UP
Join raglan seams. Join side and sleeve
seams.
Neckband
Using double-pointed 2¾mm needles and
A, K up 142 sts around neck edge.
Work 2cm K1, P1 rib in rounds.
Cast off in rib.

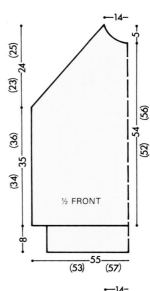

½ FRONT

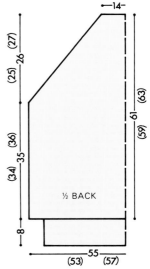

½ BACK

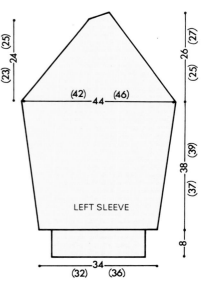

LEFT SLEEVE

Photograph: Berton   Designed by Alain Derda for Pingouin

20

Double Cream

Wrap-around jacket with patch pockets worked in double moss stitch with garter stitch borders. The yarn is a soft acrylic/cotton mixture with a slub finish.

SIZES
To fit (81)86(91)cm bust

MATERIALS
(600)650(700)g double knitting yarn
1 pair 4mm needles

TENSION
21 sts and 30 rows to 10cm over patt on 4mm needles.

RIGHT FRONT
Cast on (51)53(55) sts.
Work 2cm g st.
Commence double moss st patt inside g st border:
1st row (RS) K3, [K2, P2] to last (0)2(0) sts, K(0)2(0).
2nd row P(0)2(0), [K2, P2] to last 3 sts, K3.
3rd row K3, [P2, K2] to last (0)2(0) sts, P(0)2(0).
4th row K(0)2(0), [P2, K2] to last 3 sts, K3.
These 4 rows form the patt rep.
Cont in patt until work measures (32)33(34)cm from cast-on edge, ending with a RS row.
Shape armhole
Cast off 3 sts at beg of next row, then 2 sts at beg of foll 2 alt rows. Now dec 1 st at armhole edge on next 2 alt rows. (42)44(46) sts.
Now work straight until right front measures (49)51(53)cm from cast-on edge, ending with a RS row.
Next row Patt to last 14 sts, K to end.
Next row K14, patt to end.
Next row Patt to last 14 sts, K to end.
Shape neck
Cast off 14 sts at beg of next row, then 2 sts at beg of foll 2 alt rows. Now dec 1 st at neck edge on next 2 alt rows. (22)24(26) sts.
Work straight until armhole measures (24)25(26)cm, ending at armhole edge.
Shape shoulder
Cast off (8)8(9) sts at beg of next row and (7)8(9) sts at beg of foll alt row.
Cast off rem (7)8(8) sts.

LEFT FRONT
Work as given for right front reversing g st borders and all shapings.

BACK
Cast on (98)102(106) sts.
Work 2cm g st.
Commence double moss st patt:
1st row (RS)K2, [P2, K2] to end.
2nd row P2, [K2, P2] to end.
3rd row As 2nd row.
4th row As 1st row.
These 4 rows form the patt rep.

Cont in patt until work measures (32)33(34)cm from cast-on edge.
Shape armholes
Cast off 3 sts at beg of next 2 rows, then 2 sts at beg of foll 4 rows. Now dec 1 st at each end of next and foll alt row. (80)84(88) sts.
Work straight until armholes measure (24)25(26)cm.
Shape shoulders
Cast off (8)8(9) sts at beg of next 2 rows, then (7)8(9) sts at beg of foll 2 rows. (50)52(52) sts.
Next row Patt (7)8(8) sts, cast off 36 sts, patt to end.
Next row Cast off (7)8(8) sts, fasten off, rejoin yarn to rem sts, cast off.

SLEEVES
Cast on (58)62(66) sts.
Work 2cm g st.
Cont in patt as given for back, inc 1 st at each end of every foll 12th row until there are (76)80(84) sts.
Work straight until sleeve measures (45)46(47)cm from cast-on edge.
Shape top
Cast off 3 sts at beg of next 2 rows, then 2 sts at beg of foll 2 rows. Now dec 1 st at each end of every foll alt row until there are (34)38(42) sts. Now cast off 2 sts at beg of next (2)4(6) rows and 3 sts at beg of foll 6 rows. 12 sts.
Cast off.

COLLAR
Cast on 102 sts. Work 1cm g st.
Commence double moss st patt inside g st border:
1st row (RS) K3, [K2, P2] to last 3 sts, K3.
2nd row As 1st row.
3rd row K3, [P2, K2] to last 3 sts, K3.
4th row As 3rd row.
These 4 rows form patt rep.
Cont in patt, inc 1 st inside g st borders at each end of next and 2 foll 4th rows. 108 sts.
Work straight until collar measures 7cm from cast-on edge.
Cast off.

POCKETS (make 2)
Cast on 26 sts. Work 1cm g st.
Cont in patt as given for collar until work measures 8cm from cast-on edge.
Work 1cm g st.
Cast off.

MAKING UP
Join shoulder seams and side seams.
Join sleeve seams and set in sleeves.
Sew a pocket on to each front, 6cm in from the side seams and just above the g st border. Join on collar.

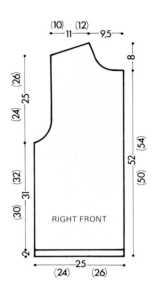

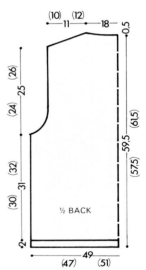

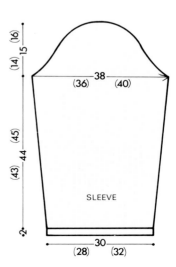

Photograph: Simpson   Designed by Françoise Gilbert

Matelot

A boxy jacket with a sailor collar made in twisted rib and twisted stocking stitch in a smooth plain wool/acrylic yarn.

SPRING
★

SIZE
To fit 81–91cm bust

MATERIALS
550g double knitting yarn
1 pair each 2¾mm, 3¼mm and 3¾mm needles

TENSION
24 sts and 28 rows to 10cm over twisted st st on 3¾mm needles.

RIGHT FRONT
Using 2¾mm needles, cast on 64 sts.
Work in twisted K1, P1 rib:
1st row (RS) *K1 tbl, P1; rep from * to end of row.
This row forms twisted rib patt rep.
Cont in twisted rib until rib measures 2cm, ending with a WS row.
Change to 3¾mm needles and cont in twisted st st:
1st row (RS) K tbl to end.
2nd row P to end.
These 2 rows form patt rep.
Cont in twisted st st until work measures 23cm from top of twisted rib, ending with a RS row.
Shape armhole and neck
Cast off 12 sts at beg of next row, now dec 1 st at armhole edge on foll 5 alt rows, *at the same time*, when work measures 25cm from top of rib, dec 1 st at neck edge on next and every foll 3rd row until 31 sts rem.
Now work straight until armhole measures 23cm.
Cast off.

LEFT FRONT
Work as given for right front reversing all shapings.

BACK
Using 2¾mm needles cast on 132 sts.
Work 2cm twisted K1, P1 rib as given for right front, ending with a WS row.
Change to 3¾mm needles. Cont in twisted st st as given for right front of jacket until work measures 23cm from top of rib.
Shape armholes
Cast off 12 sts at beg of next 2 rows, then dec 1 st at each end of next and foll 4 alt rows. 98 sts.
Now work straight until armhole measures 23cm.
Cast off.

SLEEVES
Using 2¾mm needles, cast on 64 sts.
Work 2.5cm twisted K1, P1 rib as given for right front.
Change to 3¾mm needles and cont in twisted st st as given for right front, inc 1 st at each end of every foll 6th row until there are 106 sts.
Now work straight until sleeve measures 48cm from top of rib.
Shape top
Dec 1 st at each end of next and foll 4 alt rows. 96 sts.
Cast off.

COLLAR AND FRONT BANDS
Right and left front collar made separately to back neck.
Shape right collar and front band
Using 3¼mm needles, cast on 10 sts.
Work 27cm twisted K1, P1 rib, ending with a RS row.
Work 1 row. Inc 1 st at the end of next and foll 4th row.
Rep from ** to ** 12 times more. 36 sts.
Now work straight until work measures 54cm from cast-on edge, ending with a RS row.***
Leave these sts on a spare needle.
Shape left collar and front band
Using 3¼mm needles, cast on 10 sts.
Work 27cm twisted K1, P1 rib, ending with a WS row.
Now work from ** to *** as given for right collar and neckband.
Commence back collar:
Next row Rib 36, turn, and cast on 52 sts, turn, rib 36 from spare needle. 124 sts.
Cont in twisted K1, P1 rib until work measures 74cm from cast-on edge.
Cast off in rib.

MAKING UP
Join shoulder seams.
Join side and sleeve seams and set in sleeves. Sew collar and front bands to neck and front edges.

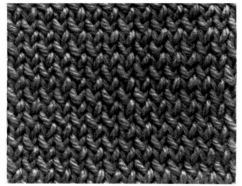

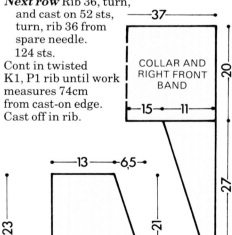

COLLAR AND RIGHT FRONT BAND

37
15 — 11
20
27
27

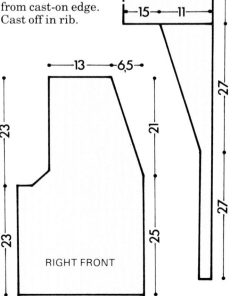

13 — 6.5
23
21
23
25
2
RIGHT FRONT
26

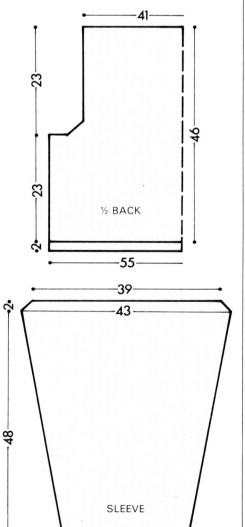

41
23
46
23
½ BACK
2
55

39
2
43
48
SLEEVE
26

Photograph: Sepp   Designed by Valérie Ribadeau Dumas

V-Yoked Sweater

A beautifully styled sweater with a V-shaped ribbed yoke, double pocket and a drawstring hem.

SPRING
★ ★

SIZES
To fit (81)86(91)cm bust

MATERIALS
(650)650(700)g Aran-weight yarn
1 pair each 4mm and 5mm needles
1 each 4½mm and 5mm circular needle

TENSION
18 sts and 22 rows to 10cm over Irish moss st on 5mm needles.

IRISH MOSS ST
[Over an odd (even) number of sts]
1st row (RS)K1(0), [P1, K1] to end.
2nd row K all the P sts of previous row and P all the K sts.
3rd row P1(0), [K1, P1] to end.
4th row K all the P sts of previous row and P all the K sts.
These 4 rows form patt rep.

FRONT
Using 4mm needles, cast on (87)91(95) sts.
Work 4cm K1, P1 rib, ending with a RS row. Make eyelet on next row:
Next row Rib 4, yrn, work 2 tog, rib to end of row.
Cont in rib until work measures 8cm from beg, ending with a WS row.
Change to 5mm needles and cont in Irish moss st:
Next row Patt (16)17(18) sts, sl next (55)57(59) sts on to spare needle for top of pocket and hold at front of work, turn, cast on (55)57(59) sts, turn, patt across rem (16)17(18) sts. (87)91(95) sts.
Cont in Irish moss st until work measures 16cm from top of rib, ending with a 2nd patt row.
Next row Patt (16)17(18) sts, cast off (55)57(59) sts, patt to end.
Leave both sets of sts on st holders and return to sts left on spare needle for pocket top.
With RS of work facing, using 5mm needles rejoin yarn to next st.
Next row K5, work in Irish moss st to last 5 sts, K5.
Rep last row until pocket top measures 16cm, ending with a 3rd patt row, leave these sts on a spare needle. Return to sts on st holder at LH side of front.
Using 5mm needles, with WS of work facing, rejoin yarn to next st.
Next row Patt (16)17(18) sts, patt across pocket top sts, patt (16)17(18) sts across st holder at RH front. (87)91(95) sts.
Cont in Irish moss at until work measures (32)34(36)cm from top of rib, ending with a WS row.
Commence yoke:
Next row Patt (42)44(46), P1, K1, P1, patt to end.

Next row Patt (42)44(46), K1, P1, K1, patt to end.
Next row Patt (40)42(44), K1, P2, K1, P2, K1, patt to end.
Next row Patt (40)42(44) P1, K2, P1, K2, P1, patt to end.
Next row Patt (39)41(43), P1, K1, P2, K1, P2, K1, P1, patt to end.
Next row Patt (39)41(43) K1, P1, K2, P1. K2, P1, K1, patt to end.
Cont in this way, working 2 more sts and 1 more st alternately in K1, P2 rib on each side of yoke on every alt row until 21 sts have been worked in rib, ending with a WS row.
Shape armholes
Cont to inc rib sts as before, cast off (4)5(6) sts at beg of next 2 rows, then (2)3(4) sts at beg of foll 2 rows, now dec 1 st at each end of next and every alt row until 57 sts rem.
Leave these sts on a spare needle.

BACK
Using 4mm needles, cast on (87)91(95) sts.
Work 4cm K1, P1 rib, ending with a WS row. Make eyelet on next row:
Next row Rib 4, yrn, work 2 tog, rib to end of row.
Cont in rib until work measures 8cm from beg, ending with a WS row.
Change to 5mm needles and cont in Irish moss st until back measures same as front to armholes, ending with a WS row.
Shape armholes
Cast off (4)5(6) sts at beg of next 2 rows, and (2)3(4) sts at beg of foll 2 rows, now dec 1 st at each end of next and 4 foll alt rows. 65 sts.
Work 1 row. Commence yoke:

Next row Work 2 tog, patt 24 sts, [K1, P2] 4 times, K1, patt to last 2 sts, work 2 tog. 63 sts.
Cont to dec 1 st at each end of next 3 alt rows, *at the same time*, work 3 more sts into K1, P2 rib at each side of yoke on next row and 4 sts into rib at each side of yoke on foll row.
Cont in this way until 57 sts rem.
Leave these sts on a spare needle.

SLEEVES
Using 4mm needles, cast on (43)47(51) sts.
Work 6cm K1, P1 rib.
Change to 5mm needles and cont in Irish moss st, inc 1 st each end of every foll 10th row until there are (59)61(65) sts.
Work straight until sleeve measures (40)42(44)cm from top of rib.
Shape top
Cast off (4)5(6) sts at beg of next 2 rows, then (2)3(4) sts at beg of foll 2 rows, now dec 1 st at each end of every foll alt row until 29 sts rem. Work 1 row.
Leave these sts on a spare needle.

YOKE
With RS of work facing, sl sts left at top of left sleeve, along front neck, top of right sleeve, along back neck on 5mm circular needle. Work in rounds of K1, P2 rib working last st of each piece tog with first st of next piece on first round. 168 sts.
Rib 8cm more, ending with a WS row.
Change to 4½mm circular needle and work in K1, P1 rib, working each pair of P sts tog across the first round. 112 sts.
Work 8cm K1, P1 rib.
Cast off in rib.

MAKING UP

Join armhole seams.
Join side and sleeve seams.
Catchstitch top and bottom edges of
pocket lining to front.
Fold lower rib in half inwards and
catchstitch cast-on edge to top of rib.
Make a 110cm cord and thread through
hem, bringing it out at eyelets.
Fold over yoke rib 3cm inwards and
catchstitch to neck edge.

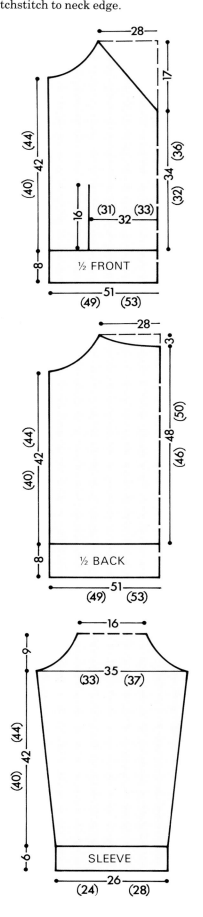

½ FRONT

28

(44) 42 (40)

17

34 (36) (32)

16 (31) (33) 32

8

51 (49) (53)

½ BACK

28

(44) 42 (40)

3

48 (50) (46)

8

51 (49) (53)

SLEEVE

16

9

35 (33) (37)

(44) 42 (40)

6

26 (24) (28)

Candy Stripe

A cap-sleeved sweater that could hardly be simpler to make. Knitted in wool rather than cotton it becomes a winter slipover.

SIZES
To fit (81)86(91)cm bust

MATERIALS
(350)350(400)g double knitting yarn in main colour (A)
(300)300(350)g in contrast colour (B)
1 pair each 3¼mm and 4½mm needles
1 set four double-pointed 3¼mm needles

TENSION
20 sts and 24 rows to 10cm over stripe patt on 4½mm needles.

FRONT
Using 3¼mm needles and A, cast on (96)100(104) sts.
Work 5cm K1, P1 rib, inc 16 sts evenly across last row. (112)116(120) sts.
Change to 4½mm needles and commence stripe patt:
1st row (RS) With A, [K1, P1] to end.
2nd row As 1st row.
3rd row With B, [P1, K1] to end.
4th row As 3rd row.
These 4 rows form patt rep.**
Cont in patt until front measures (24)25(26)cm from top of rib, ending with a WS row.
Divide for neck
Next row Patt (56)58(60), turn, leaving rem sts on a spare needle, cont on these sts only for left side of neck.
***Dec 1 st at neck edge on next and foll 13 alt rows, then on 5 foll 4th rows, at the same time, when work measures (26)27(28)cm from top of rib, inc 1 st at

armhole edge on next and 2 foll 6th rows (40)42(44) sts.
Work straight until front measures (46)48(50)cm from top of rib, ending at armhole edge.
Shape shoulder
Cast off (13)14(15) sts at beg of next and foll alt row. Work 1 row.
Cast off rem 14 sts.
Return to sts on spare needle, with RS of work facing rejoin yarn to next st.
Work 1 row.
Complete to match left side of neck working from *** to end.

BACK
Work as given for front to **.
Cont in patt until back measures (26)27(28)cm from top of rib.
Shape sleeves
Inc 1 st at each end of next and every foll 6th row until there are (118)122(126) sts.
Work straight until back measures (46)48(50)cm from top of rib, ending with a WS row.
Shape shoulders
Cast off (13)14(15) sts at beg of next 4 rows, and 14 sts at beg of foll 2 rows.
Cast off rem 38 sts.

MAKING UP
Join shoulder seams.
Neckband
Using double-pointed 3¼mm needles and A, with RS of work facing, K up (61)64(67) sts evenly down left side of neck, K up 1 st from centre front, K up (61)64(67) sts

evenly up right side of neck and 37 sts across back neck. (160)166(172) sts.
Work in K1, P1 rib making centre st at front 'V' a K st. Rib 8 rounds, P2 tog on either side of centre st on each round. (144)150(156) sts.
Next round Rib (12)13(14), cast off (83)87(91) sts, rib to end.
Change to 4½mm needles and cont in rows on rem (61)63(65) sts for collar.
Work in K1, P1 rib, inc 1 st at each end of next and every foll 4th row until there are (73)75(77) sts. Work straight until work measures 13cm from K up round.
Cast off loosely in rib.
Armbands
Using 3¼mm needles and A, with RS of work facing, K up (102)106(110) sts around armhole edge.
Work 2cm K1, P1 rib. Cast off in rib.
Join side seams.

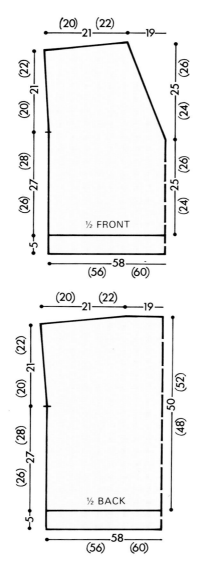

Photograph: G. Vidon   Designed by Josiane Routoure

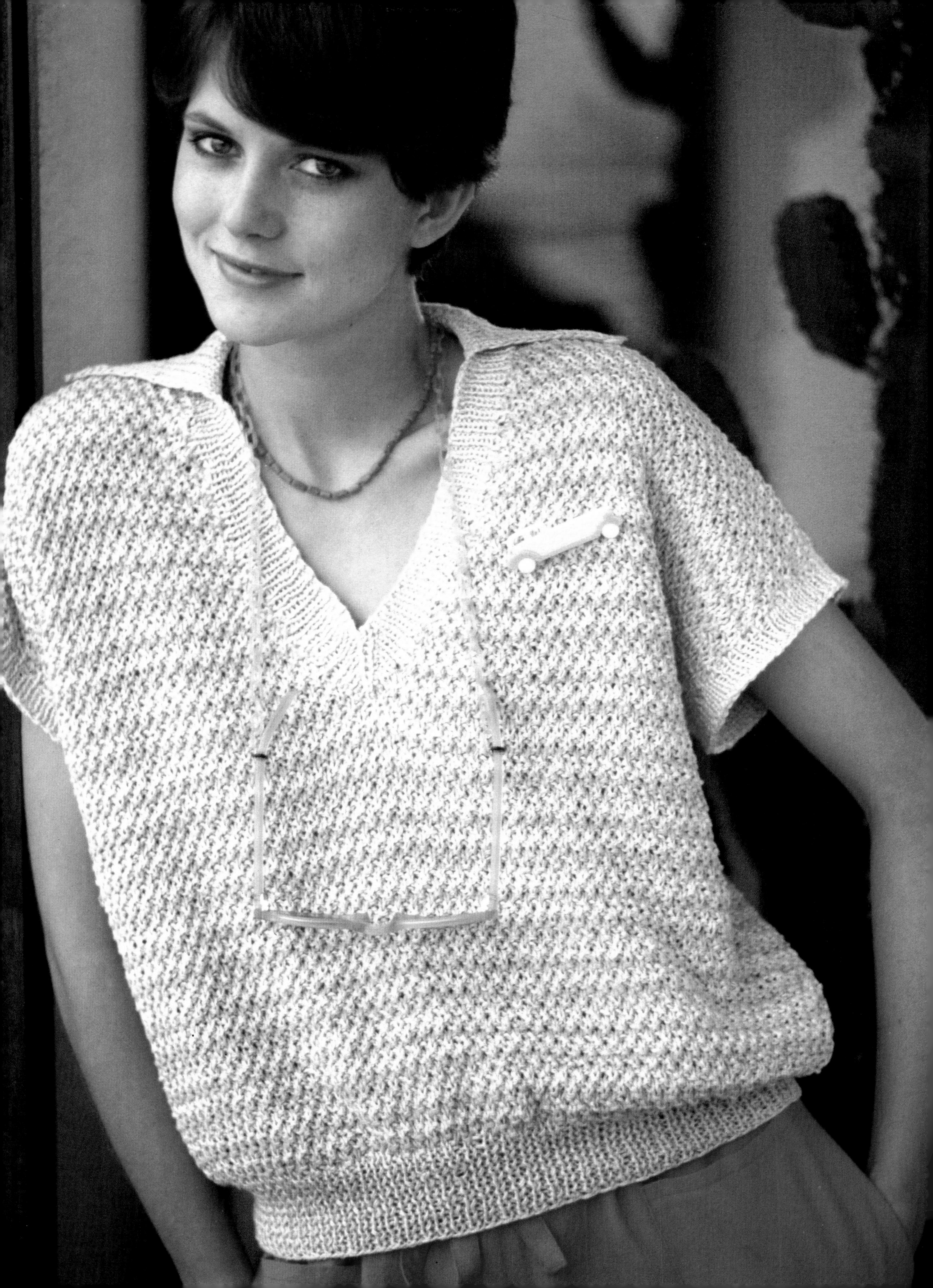

Cool Cotton

A longline sweater with a zigzag pattern picked out in purl stitches worked on the front only. It is made in a cotton yarn used double or you can make a winter version in chunky wool.

SIZES
To fit (81)86(91)cm bust

MATERIALS
(700)700(750)g double knitting yarn
1 pair 7mm needles

TENSION
13 sts and 17 rows to 10cm over patt on 7mm needles using yarn double.

FRONT
Using yarn double, cast on (62)64(66) sts.
Work (5)6(7)cm K1, P1 rib.
Commence patt:
1st row (RS) *K3, P2; rep from * to last (2)4(1) sts, (K2)K3, P1(K1)
2nd row (P1, K1)P3, K1(K1), *K1, P3, K1; rep from * to end.
3rd row *P2, K3; rep from * to last (2)4(1) sts, (P2)P2, K2(P1).
4th row (K1, P1)P1, K2, P1(P1), *P2, K2, P1; rep from * to end.
These four rows establish the patt. Cont in this way moving the P sts one st to the left on RS rows and one st to the right on WS rows until 18 patt rows in all have been worked.
Next row K the P sts of previous row and P the K sts.
Now reverse the diagonals by moving the P sts one st to the right on RS rows and one st to the left on WS rows until 36 patt rows in all have been worked.
These 36 rows form the patt rep. Cont in patt until work measures 34cm from top of rib, ending with a WS row.
Shape armholes
Cast off 6 sts at beg of next 2 rows.
(50)52(54) sts.
Cont in patt until 72 rows in all have been worked from top of rib.**
Work (9)10(11)cm K1, P1 rib.
Cast off in rib.

BACK
Using yarn double, cast on (46)48(50) sts.
Work (5)6(7)cm K1, P1 rib.
Cont in st st until back matches front to **, ending with a P row.
Work (9)10(11)cm K1, P1 rib.
Cast off in rib.

SLEEVES
Using yarn double, cast on (28)30(32) sts.
Work 10cm K1, P1 rib.
Now work in st st, inc 1 st at each end of every foll 8th row until there are (44)46(48) sts.
Cont in st st until work measures (43)44(45)cm from top of rib.
Cast off.

MAKING UP
Mark neck opening 12cm in on each side of back and front.
Join shoulder seams.
Join side and sleeve seams.
Set in sleeves.
Fold back cuffs.

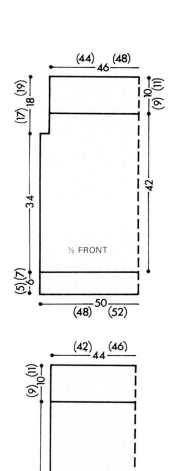

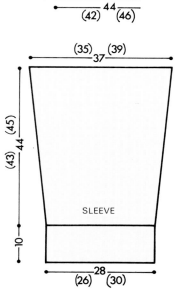

30

Photograph: Sacha   Designed by Marie-José-Flosy for Fac Bazaar

T-Shirt

The motifs on this T-shaped top are Swiss-darned on after the main work is completed. To make things even easier it is worked all in one piece from the lower front edge to the lower back edge.

SUMMER
★ ★

SIZES
To fit (81)86(91)cm bust

MATERIALS
(300)350(400)g double knitting yarn in main colour (A)
50g in each of 3 contrast colours (B, C, D)
1 pair 3¾mm needles
1 3.00mm crochet hook

TENSION
24 sts and 35 rows to 10cm over st st on 3¾mm needles.

TO MAKE (one piece)
Beg at lower edge front, using A, cast on (110)116(122) sts.
Work in st st until front measures (22)23(24)cm, ending with a WS row.
Shape sleeves
Cast on (60)63(66) sts at beg of next 2 rows. (230)242(254) sts.
Cont in st st until work measures (38)40(42)cm from the beg, ending with a WS row.
Divide for neck
Next row K(90)96(102) sts, turn, leaving rem sts on a spare needle, cont on these sts only for left side of neck and left sleeve.
Work 10cm st st without shaping, ending with a RS row, leave these sts on a second spare needle.
Return to sts on first spare needle, with RS facing rejoin A to next st, cast off 50 sts, cont on rem (90)96(102) sts for right side of neck and right sleeve.
Work 10cm st st without shaping, ending with a RS row.
Next row P to end, turn, cast on 50 sts, turn, P across sts held on second spare needle. (230)242(254) sts.
Next row K to end across all sts.
Cont in st st until sleeve measures (42)44(46)cm from beg of shaping.
Shape back
Cast off (60)63(66) sts at beg of next 2 rows. (110)116(122) sts.
Work (22)23(24)cm st st, ending with a WS row.
Cast off.

MAKING UP
Using A, work 1 row double crochet round neck edge.
Swiss-darn motifs on back, front and sleeves using contrast colours B, C and D, as shown on chart. (See page 123 for working Swiss darning.)
Join side and sleeve seams.
Work 1 row double crochet in A or in any of the contrast colours around edges of sleeves and body.

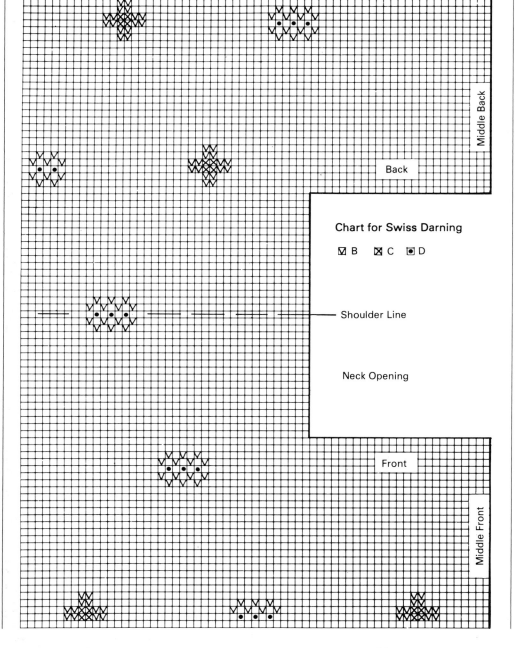

Chart for Swiss Darning

☑ B   ☒ C   ⊡ D

Shoulder Line

Neck Opening

Back

Front

Middle Back

Middle Front

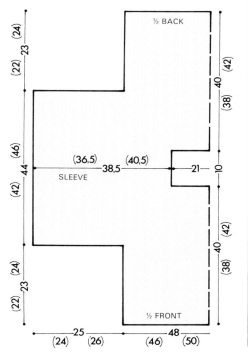

½ BACK

SLEEVE

½ FRONT

(22) 23 (24)
(46) 44 (42)
(22) 23 (24)
(36,5) — 38,5 — (40,5)
21 — 10
25 (24) (26)
48 (46) (50)
40 (42) (38)
40 (42) (38)

Photograph: Hibbs   Designed by Françoise Gilbert

Cotton Tweed

Two contrast-coloured thinner yarns twisted together would give the same effect as the heavy tweedy cotton used in this short-sleeved cardigan which is made all in one piece.

SIZES
To fit (81)86(91)cm bust

MATERIALS
(500)500(550)g Aran-weight yarn
1 pair each 4mm and 5mm needles
5 buttons

TENSION
18 sts and 25 rows to 10cm over patt on 5mm needles.

TO MAKE (one piece)
Beg at lower edge back, using 4mm needles, cast on (76)80(84) sts.
Work 5cm twisted K2, P2 rib (work K sts tbl), dec 1 st in centre of last row.
Change to 5mm needles and commence patt:
1st row (RS) (P5)K1, P6(P1, K2, P6), [K2, P6] 4 times, K1, [P6, K2] 4 times, (P5)P6, K1(P6, K2, P1).
2nd row K all the P sts of previous row and P all the K sts, inc 1 st at each end of row.
3rd row (P5, K1)K1, P6, K1(P1, K2, P6, K1), [K1, P6, K1] 4 times, K1, [K1, P6, K1] 4 times, (K1, P5)K1, P6, K1(K1, P6, K2, P1).
4th row K all the P sts of previous row and P all the K sts, inc 1 st at each end of row.
These 4 rows set the position of the patt.
Cont in patt working centre sts from chart, moving the P sts on every alt row 1 st to the right on RH side of work and 1 st to the left on LH side of work, *at the same time*, inc 1 st at each end of every alt row until there are (123)129(135) sts, ending with a WS row.
Shape sleeve
Cast on 8 sts at beg of next 2 rows. (139)145(151) sts.
Cont in patt, but working the 8 sts at each side for sleeves in horizontal rib (alt 1 row K, 2 rows P).
Work straight until back measures (36)38(40)cm from top of rib, ending with a WS row.
Divide for neck
Next row Patt (51)54(57) sts, leave these sts on a spare needle, patt 37 sts, turn, leaving rem sts on second spare needle, cont on these sts only for neckband.
Change to 4mm needles and work 4 rows twisted K2, P2 rib, dec 1 st at centre of 1st row. 36 sts.
Cast off loosely in rib.
Change to 5mm needles and return to sts on second spare needle, with RS of work facing rejoin yarn to next st.
Shape left side
Cont in patt, working sts for left sleeve in horizontal rib as before, but also working

4 sts on RH side in horizontal rib for front border, until work measures (44)47(50)cm from top of rib.
Cont in patt and borders as set, inc 1 st inside front border sts on next and every foll 3rd row until work measures (55)58(61)cm from top of rib.
Now reverse the patt, moving the P sts on every alt row 1 st to the right instead of left on the LH side of the work (and 1 st to the right on the RH side of the work).
Keeping incs correct, cont in patt until sleeve border edge measures (40)42(44)cm, ending at sleeve edge.
Next row Cast off 8 sts, patt to end.
Make buttonhole:
1st buttonhole row Patt 2 sts, cast off 2 sts, patt to last 2 sts, work 2 tog.
2nd buttonhole row Patt to end, casting on 2 sts over those cast off in previous row.
Keeping incs inside front border correct, cont in patt making 4 more buttonholes as before at (5)5.5(6)cm intervals, *at the same time* dec 1 st at beg of next and every foll alt row (side seam edge) until 19 incs in all have been made inside front border.
Now cont in patt, making buttonholes and dec at side seam edge as set, but working front opening edge straight until (24)25(26) decs in all have been worked at side seam edge. (38)40(42) sts.
Change to 4mm needles and, keeping horizontal rib border correct, work 5cm twisted K2, P2 rib.

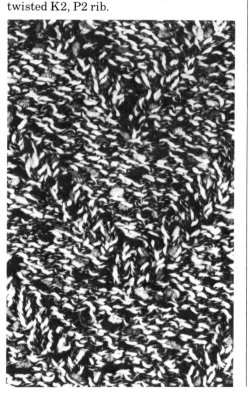

Cast off loosely in rib.
Return to sts on first spare needle, using 5mm needles, rejoin yarn to sts at neck edge and work right side to match left side reversing all shapings, patt and omitting buttonholes.

MAKING UP
Join side and underarm seams.
Catch down back neck border to side borders.
Sew on buttons.

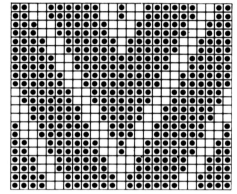

● P □ K

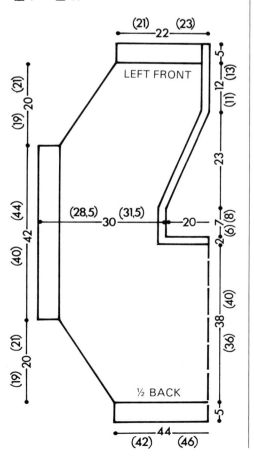

Photograph: A. Carrara Designed by Françoise Gilbert for Fac Bazaar

Hearts and Flowers

Equally effective in wool or cotton, this pretty cardigan has patterned fronts and a plain back and sleeves.

SIZES
To fit age (4)6(8) years

MATERIALS
(200)250(300)g four-ply yarn in main colour (A)
50g in each of 6 contrast colours (B, C, D, E, F, G)
1 pair 2¼mm needles
1 pair 3mm needles
5 buttons

TENSION
27 sts and 34 rows to 10cm over st st on 3mm needles.

RIGHT FRONT
Using 2¼mm needles and A, cast on (39)42(45) sts.
Work 6cm K1, P1 rib, inc 8 sts evenly across last row. (47)50(53) sts.
Change to 3mm needles and work 2 rows st st.**
Commence flower patt from chart:
1st row (RS) *K3A, 1B, 3A; rep from * to last (5)1(4) sts, (3A, 1B, 1A)1A(3A, 1B).
2nd row P(3B, 2A)1A(2B, 2A), *2A, 3B, 2A; rep from * to end.
These 2 rows set the position of the chart patt.
Cont in patt until work measures (20)22(24)cm from top of rib, ending with a RS row.
Shape armhole and neck edge
Cast off 5 sts at beg of next row and 2 sts at beg of foll alt row.
Now dec 1 st at beg of foll 2 alt rows, *at the same time*, when work measures (20)23(26)cm from top of rib, dec 1 st at neck edge on next and every foll alt row until (18)21(24) sts rem.
Work straight until armhole measures (14)15(16)cm from beg, ending at armhole edge. Cast off.

LEFT FRONT
Work as given for right front to **.
Commence flower patt from chart:
1st row (RS) K(1A, 1B, 3A)1A(1B, 3A), *3A, 1B, 3A; rep from * to end.
2nd row *P2A, 3B, 2A; rep from * to last (5)1(4) sts, (2A, 3B)1A(2A, 2B).
These 2 rows set the position of the chart patt.
Complete as given for right front reversing all shapings.

BACK
Using 2¼mm needles and A, cast on (74)80(86) sts.
Work 6cm K1, P1 rib.
Change to 3mm needles and cont in st st until work measures (20)22(24)cm from top of rib.

Shape armholes
Cast off 3 sts at beg of next 2 rows, then dec 1 st at each end of foll 2 alt rows. (64)70(76) sts.
Work straight until back measures 4 rows less than left front to shoulder, ending with a WS row.
Divide for neck
Next row Patt (23)26(29) sts, turn, leaving rem sts on a spare needle, cont on these sts only for first side of neck.
Work 2 rows. Cast off 5 sts at beg of next row. (18)21(24) sts.
Cast off.
Return to sts on spare needle, with RS of work facing, rejoin yarn to next st, cast off 18 sts, patt to end.
Work 3 rows.
Complete to match first side of neck reversing shaping.

SLEEVES
Using 2¼mm needles and A, cast on (44)50(56) sts.
Work 4cm K1, P1 rib.
Change to 3mm needles and cont in st st, inc 1 st at each end of every foll 8th row until there are (56)62(68) sts.
Work straight until sleeve measures (24)26(28)cm from top of rib.
Shape top
Cast off 3 sts at beg of next 2 rows, then 2 sts at beg of foll 4 rows.
Now dec 1 st at each end of next and 12 foll alt rows.
Cast off 2 sts at beg of foll (2)4(6) rows and 3 sts at beg of foll 2 rows.
Cast off rem (6)8(10) sts.

FRONT AND NECK BORDER
Using 2¼mm needles and A, cast on 11 sts.
Work (1.5)2(2.5)cm K1, P1 rib.
Make buttonhole:
1st buttonhole row Rib 4, cast off 3 sts, rib to end.
2nd buttonhole row Rib to end, casting on 3 sts over those cast off in previous row.
Cont in rib, making 4 more buttonholes at (4.5)5(5.5)cm intervals, until work measures (97)100(103)cm or until border, when slightly stretched, fits up right front across back neck and down left front of cardigan.
Cast off in rib.

MAKING UP
Join shoulder seams. Sew on front and neck border, joining buttonhole section to right front.
Join side and sleeve seams.
Set in sleeves.
Sew on buttons.

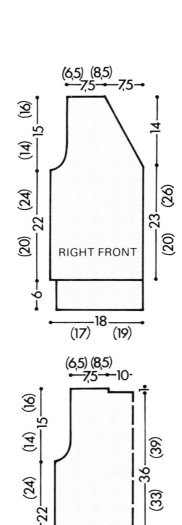

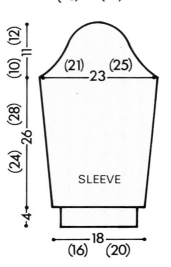

Photograph: M. Yavel   Designed by Soizic Cornu for Fac Bazaar

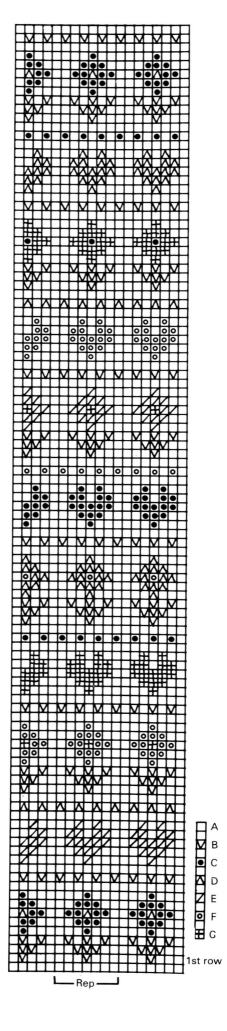

A
B
C
D
E
F
G

1st row

Rep

Diagonal Rib

A longline sweater with cunningly
constructed sleeves. In some parts
the fine yarn is used double, in
others three strands are twisted
together. For a stunning variation
use different coloured strands.

SIZES
To fit (81)86(91)cm bust

MATERIALS
(700)750(800)g four-ply yarn
1 pair each 4mm, 4½mm, 6mm and 7mm
needles

TENSION
14 sts and 18 rows to 10cm over patt on
7mm needles using 3 strands of yarn
together.

FRONT
Using 6mm needles and 3 strands of yarn
tog, cast on (63)66(69) sts.
Work 5cm K1, P1 rib.
Change to 7mm needles and commence
patt:
1st row (RS) *K2, P3; rep from * to last
  (3)1(4) sts, (K2, P1)K1 (K2, P2).
2nd row K all the P sts of previous row
  and P all the K sts.
3rd row *K1, P3, K1; rep from * to last
  (3)1(4) sts, (K1, P2)K1(K1, P3).
4th row K all the P sts of previous row
  and P all the K sts.
These 4 rows establish the diagonal st
patt. Cont as set moving the P sts 1 st to
the right on every RS row.
Cont in patt until work measures
(32)33(34)cm from top of rib.
Shape armholes
Cast off 5 sts at beg of next 2 rows.
(53)56(59) sts.

Work straight until front measures
(41)43(45)cm from top of rib.
Work 20 rows g st.
Change to 6mm needles and work 3 rows
K1, P1 rib.
Cast off in rib.

BACK
Work as given for front.

SLEEVE
Using 4mm needles and 2 strands of yarn
tog, cast on (83)87(91) sts.
Work 5cm K1, P1 rib.
Change to 4½mm needles and cont in rib
until work measures 14cm from beg.
Next row Cast off (56)58(60) sts, rib to
  end. (27)29(31) sts.
Cont in rib until sleeve measures
(41)43(45)cm from beg.
Cast off in rib.

UPPER SLEEVE
Using 7mm needles and 3 strands of yarn
tog, cast on (38)40(42) sts.
Work (25)26(27)cm g st. Cast off.

MAKING UP
Join shoulder seams to (3)4(5)cm in from
side edge.
Join upper sleeve to sleeve, matching row
end edge of upper sleeve to cast-off
sts at top of cuff. Set in sleeve
(reverse patt on 2nd sleeve), easing
upper sleeve edge to fit smoothly,
and joining last few rows of sleeve to
cast-off sts at underarm. Join side
and underarm seams.

Measurements across bottom of
'L'-shaped Sleeve diagram should be:
(38)40(42).

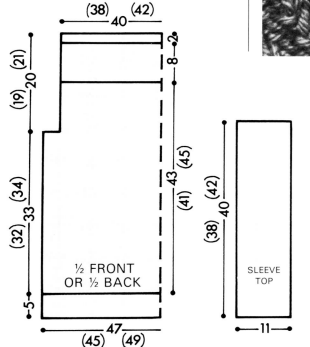

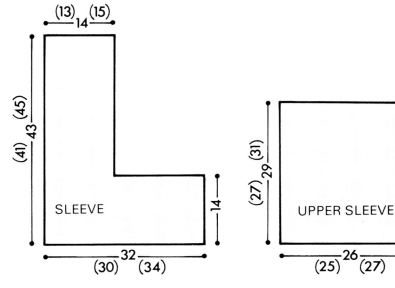

Photograph: J.-P. Metayer   Designed by Torrente

Cotton Jerkin

The perfect pattern for absolute beginners. Nothing could be simpler than this jerkin in a basketweave stitch with garter stitch edgings.

SUMMER
★

SIZES
To fit (81)86(91)cm bust

MATERIALS
(500)500(550)g double knitting yarn
1 pair 7mm needles

TENSION
12 sts and 18 rows to 10cm over basket-weave patt using yarn double.

RIGHT FRONT
Using yarn double, cast on (29)31(33) sts.
Work 6 rows g st.
Commence patt:
1st row (RS) K3, *P2, K2; rep from * to last (2)4(2) sts, (K2)P2, K2(K2).
2nd row (K2)K2, P2(K2), *K2, P2; rep from * to last 3 sts, K3.
3rd row K3, *K2, P2; rep from * to last (2)4(2) sts, K(2)4(2).
4th row K(2)4(2), *P2, K2; rep from * to last 3 sts, K3.
These 4 rows establish the basketweave patt inside g st borders. Cont in patt until work measures (29)30(31)cm from cast-on edge, ending with a WS row.
Shape neck
Next row K3, work 2 tog, patt to end of row. (28)30(32) sts.
Next row K2, patt to end.
Next row K3, work 2 tog, patt to last 8 sts, K8. (27)29(31) sts.
Next row K8, patt to end.
Next row K3, work 2 tog, patt to last 8 sts, K8. (26)28(30) sts.
Shape armhole
Next row Cast off 6 sts, K2 including st used to cast off, patt to end of row. (20)22(24) sts.
Keeping basketweave patt and g st borders correct, cont to dec at neck edge as

set on next and foll alt row, then on every foll 4th row until there are (15)17(19) sts.
Work straight until armhole measures (19)20(21)cm from beg.
Cast off.

LEFT FRONT
Work as given for right front reading RS for WS and *vice versa* throughout.

BACK
Using yarn double, cast on (46)50(54) sts.
Work 6 rows g st.
Cont in basketweave patt, working 2 sts at each end of every row in g st, until back measures 3 rows less than right front to armhole.
Next row K4, patt to last 4 sts, K4.
Rep last row twice more.
Shape armholes
Cast off 2 sts at beg of next 2 rows.
(42)46(50) sts.
Now work straight until work measures (47)49(51)cm, ending with a WS row.
Next row Patt (12)14(16), K18, patt to end.
Rep last row twice more.
Divide for neck
Next row Patt (15)17(19) sts, turn, leaving rem sts on a spare needle.
Next row K3, patt to end.
Next row Patt to last 3 sts, K3.
Cast off.
Return to sts on spare needle, with RS facing rejoin yarn to next st.
Next row Cast off 12 sts, K3 including st used to cast off, patt to end of row. (15)17(19) sts.
Complete to match first side of neck.

MAKING UP
Join shoulder seams and side seams.

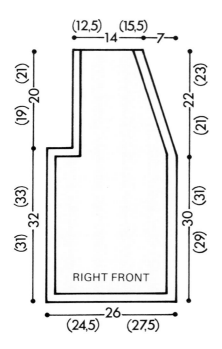

(12,5) (15,5)
14 — 7
(19)20(21)
(23)22(21)
(29)30(31)
(31)32(33)
RIGHT FRONT
26
(24,5) (27,5)

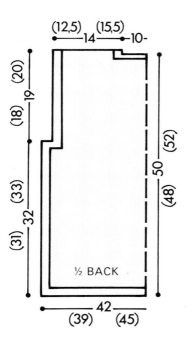

(12,5) (15,5)
14 — 10
(18)19(20)
(48)50(52)
(31)32(33)
½ BACK
42
(39) (45)

Photograph: M. Momy   Designed by Sophie Serret

Cover Up

This short-sleeved cotton cardigan is an elegant and practical antidote to cool summer evenings. Made longer, it becomes an equally stylish beach robe.

SIZES
To fit (81)86(91)cm bust

MATERIALS
(500)550(550)g Aran-weight yarn
1 pair each 4½mm and 5mm needles
3 buttons

TENSION
15 sts and 21 rows to 10cm over patt as given for back on 5mm needles.

RIGHT FRONT
Using 4½mm needles, cast on (48)50(52) sts.
Work 3cm K1, P1 rib, ending with a WS row.
1st buttonhole row Rib 3, cast off 4 sts, work to end.
2nd buttonhole row Work to end, casting on 4 sts over those cast off in previous row.
Cont in rib until work measures 7cm, ending with a WS row.
Change to 5mm needles and commence patt:
1st row (RS) Rib 11, K to end.
2nd row K to last 11 sts, rib to end.
3rd row Rib to end.
4th row Rib to end.
These 4 rows form patt rep.
Cont in patt, making 2 more buttonholes as before – one 6cm from the first one and another 6cm from the second one – until work measures (18)19(20)cm from top of rib, ending with a WS row.
Shape neck and armhole
(Work all neck decs inside 11-st rib border.)
Work 2 sts tog at neck edge on next and foll alt row then on 12 foll 3rd rows, *at the same time* cast off 3 sts at armhole edge on next alt row, 2 sts on foll alt row, then dec 1 st at armhole edge on 3 foll alt rows. (26)28(30) sts.
Work straight until armhole measures (22)23(24)cm, ending at armhole edge.
Shape shoulder
Cast off (5)6(7) sts beg of next and foll alt row, then 5 sts at beg of next alt row. 11 sts.**
Shape back neck border
Cont in K1, P1 rib for 15cm.
Cast off in rib.

LEFT FRONT
Work as given for right front to **, omitting buttonholes and reversing rib border and all shapings.
Cast off in rib.

BACK
Using 4½mm needles, cast on (68)72(76) sts. Work 7cm K1, P1 rib, ending with a WS row. Change to 5mm needles and commence patt:
1st row (RS) K to end.
2nd row As 1st row.
3rd row [K1, P1] to end.
4th row As 3rd row.
These 4 rows form patt rep. Cont in patt until back measures (18)19(20)cm from top of rib.
Shape armholes
Cast off 3 sts at beg of next 2 rows, then 2 sts at beg of foll 2 rows.
Dec 1 st at each end of foll 2 alt rows. (54)58(62) sts.
Work straight until armhole measures (22)23(24)cm, ending with a WS row.
Divide for neck
Next row Patt (21)23(25) sts, turn, leaving rem sts on a spare needle, cont on these sts only for right side of neck.
Shape neck and shoulder
Cast off 3 sts at beg of next row, (5)6(7) sts at beg of foll row, 2 sts at beg of next row and (5)6(7) sts at beg of next row.
Cast off rem 6 sts.
Return to sts on spare needle, with RS of work facing rejoin yarn to next st.
Next row Cast off 12 sts, patt to end.
Work 1 row.
Complete to match first side of neck.

SLEEVES
Using 4½mm needles, cast on (46)50(54) sts.
Work 3cm K1, P1 rib.
Change to 5mm needles and cont in patt as given for back, inc 1 st at each end of every foll 6th row until there are (52)56(60) sts.
Work straight until work measures (11)12(13)cm from top of rib.
Shape top
Cast off 3 sts at beg of next 2 rows, then 2 sts at beg of foll 2 rows.
Dec 1 st at each end of the foll (8)10(12) alt rows.
Cast off 2 sts at beg of next 8 rows.
Cast off rem 10 sts.

MAKING UP
Join shoulder seams.
Join back neck border to back neck. Join neck border seam. Join side and sleeve seams.
Set in sleeves.
Sew on buttons.

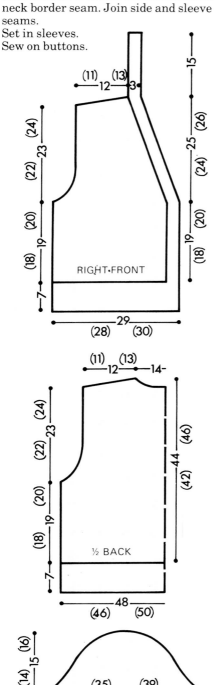

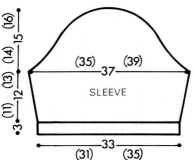

Photograph: A. Chatelain   Designed by Caroline Freese

Gold and Diamonds

All that glitters here is the lurex mixture used to highlight a diamond seed-stitch pattern. The sweater is worked in one piece, beginning at the lower front edge and ending at the lower back edge.

SUMMER
★ ★

SIZE
To fit 81–86cm bust

MATERIALS
650g double knitting yarn (A)
50g lurex mixture (B) (use fine yarn double if necessary)
1 pair 3mm and 3¾mm needles
1 set four double-pointed 3mm needles

TENSION
22 sts and 32 rows to 10cm over patt on 3¾mm needles.

TO MAKE (one piece)
Beg at lower front edge, using 3mm needles and A, cast on 105 sts.
Work 6cm K1, P1 rib, inc 16 sts evenly across last row. 121 sts.
Change to 3¾mm needles and commence diamond patt from chart:
1st row (RS) With A, [P1, K1] twice, P1, *[K1, P1] 5 times, K1, K1B, with A, [K1, P1] 5 times; rep from * to last 6 sts, [K1, P1] 3 times.
2nd row With A, [P1, K1] 3 times, *[P1, K1] 4 times, P1, P1B, P1A, P1B, with A, [P1, K1] 5 times; rep from * to last 5 sts, [P1, K1] twice, P1.
3rd row With A, [P1, K1] twice, P1, *[K1, P1] 4 times, K1, K1B, K1A, P1A, K1A, K1B, with A, [K1, P1] 4 times; rep from * to last 6 sts, [K1, P1] 3 times.
4th row With A, [P1, K1] 3 times, *[P1, K1] 3 times, P1, P1B, with A, [P1, K1] twice, P1, P1B, with A, [P1, K1] 4 times; rep from * to last 5 sts, [P1, K1] twice, P1.
These 4 rows establish the patt. Cont in patt working from chart until work measures 25cm from top of rib.
Shape sleeves
Keeping diamond patt correct, inc 1 st at each end of next and foll 7 alt rows. 137 sts.
Now cast on 2 sts at beg of next 4 rows, then 3 sts at beg of foll 10 rows, then 10 sts at beg of foll 6 rows, and 13 sts at beg of foll 4 rows. 287 sts.
Work straight in patt until sweater measures 39cm from top of rib, ending with a WS row.
Divide for neck
Next row Patt 135 sts, turn, leaving rem sts on a length of yarn, cont on these sts only for left side of neck.
Shape left front neck
Cast off 2 sts at neck edge on next and foll 12 alt rows. 109 sts.
Now work straight until front measures 49cm from top of rib. *This point marks the shoulder line.*
Shape left back neck
Work left back neck as a mirror image of left front neck from the shoulder line,

working 2cm straight then casting on sts instead of casting off.
When back neck incs are completed (135 sts on needle), end with a RS row ** and leave these sts on a spare needle.
Return to sts left on length of yarn, with RS of work facing, rejoin yarn to next st, cast off 17 sts, patt to end. 135 sts.
Work right front and back neck to match left front and back neck to **, reversing all shapings.
Join back neck
Next row Patt 135 sts, turn and cast on 17 sts, turn, patt 135 sts from spare needle. 287 sts.
Work straight until sweater measures 61cm from top of rib.
Shape back
Cast off 13 sts at beg of next 4 rows, 10 sts at beg of foll 6 rows, 3 sts at beg of foll 10 rows and 2 sts at beg of foll 4 rows. Now dec 1 st at each end of next and foll 7 alt

rows. 121 sts.
Work straight until back matches front to top of rib, dec 16 sts evenly across last row. 105 sts.
Change to 3mm needles and work 6cm K1, P1 rib.
Cast off in rib.

MAKING UP
Sleeve bands
Using 3mm needles and A, K up 59 sts from sleeve edge.
Work 6.5cm K1, P1 rib.
Change to B. Rib 1 row.
Cast off in rib in B.
Neckband
Using double-pointed 3mm needles and A, K up 148 sts around neck edge.
Work 8 rounds K1, P1 rib.
Change to B and rib 1 round.
Cast off in rib in B.
Join side and sleeve seams.

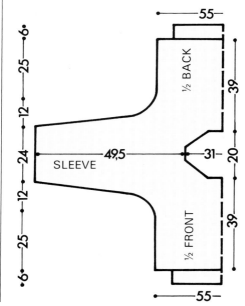

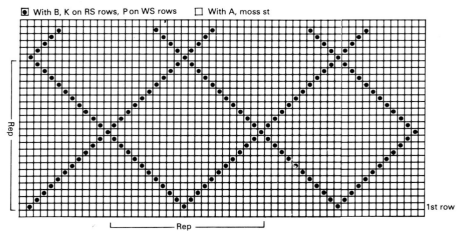

□ With B, K on RS rows, P on WS rows   □ With A, moss st

Rep

Rep

1st row

Photograph: Gourou   Designed by Jacqueline Laguilhaumie

Slash Neck

There's very little shaping and only knit and purl stitches involved in this diagonal stitch sweater worked in three strands of double knitting together.

SIZES
To fit (81)86(91)cm bust

MATERIALS
(900)950(1000)g double knitting yarn
1 pair 6mm and 7mm needles

TENSION
12 sts and 18 rows to 10cm over patt on 7mm needles using 3 strands of yarn tog.

FRONT
Using 6mm needles and 3 strands of yarn tog, cast on (53)55(57) sts.
Work 8cm K1, P1 rib, beg RS rows with P st on 1st and 3rd sizes, and K st on 2nd size, ending with a RS row.
Next row (Rib 5, make 1 by picking up loop between last st and next st and working it tbl) twice, rib to last 10 sts, (make 1, rib 5) twice. (57)59(61) sts.
Change to 7mm needles and commence patt:
1st row (RS) (P1) K1, P1(K2, P1), [K2, P1] 6 times, [K1, P1] 9 times, K1, [P1, K2] 6 times, (P1)P1, K1(P1, K2).
2nd row (P1)P2(K1, P2), [K1, P2] 6 times, [P1, K1] 9 times, P1, [P2, K1] 6 times, (P1)P2(P2, K1).
3rd row (K1)P1, K1(K1, P1, K1), [K1, P1, K1] 6 times, [K1, P1] 9 times, K1, [K1, P1, K1] 6 times, (K1) K1, P1(K1, P1, K1).
4th row (K1)P1, K1(P2, K1), [P2, K1] 6 times, [P1, K1] 9 times, P1, [K1, P2] 6 times, (K1)K1, P1(K1, P2).
5th row (K1)K2(P1, K2), [P1, K2] 6 times, [K1, P1] 9 times, K1, [K2, P1] 6 times, (K1)K2(K2, P1).
6th row (P1)K1, P1(P1, K1, P1), [P1, K1, P1] 6 times, [P1, K1] 9 times, P1, [P1, K1, P1] 6 times, (P1)P1, K1(P1, K1, P1).
These 6 rows form the patt rep.
Cont in patt, inc 1 st at each end of 2 foll 12th rows. (61)63(65) sts.
Work straight until front measures (36)37(38)cm from top of rib, ending with a WS row.
Shape armholes
Cast off 3 sts at beg of next 2 rows. (55)57(59) sts.
Cont in patt until front measures (41)43(45)cm from top of rib, ending with a WS row.
Work 10cm K1, P1 rib, beg RS rows with K st on 1st and 3rd sizes, and P st on 2nd size, ending with a WS row.
Cast off in rib.

BACK
Using 6mm needles and 3 strands of yarn tog, cast on (51)53(55) sts.
Work 8cm K1, P1 rib, inc 8 sts evenly across last row. (59)61(63) sts.

Change to 7mm needles and work in patt:
1st row (RS) [P1, K2] (19)20(21) times, (P1, K1)P1(0).
2nd row P(2)1(0), [K1, P2] (19)20(21) times.
3rd row [K1, P1, K1] (19)20(21) times, (K1, P1)K1(0).
4th row (P1, K1)K1(0), [P2, K1] (19)20(21) times.
5th row [K2, P1] (19)20(21) times, K(2)1(0).
6th row (K1, P1)P1(0), [P1, K1, P1] (19)20(21) times.
These 6 rows form the patt rep.
Cont in patt until back measures (36)37(38)cm from top of rib, ending with a WS row.
Shape armholes
Cast off 3 sts at beg of next 2 rows. (53)55(57) sts.
Work straight until back measures (41)43(45)cm from top of rib.
Work 10cm K1, P1 rib.
Cast off in rib.

RIGHT SLEEVE
Using 6mm needles and 3 strands of yarn tog, cast on (25)27(29) sts.
Work 11cm K1, P1 rib, inc 4 sts evenly across last row. (29)31(33) sts.**
Change to 7mm needles and cont in patt:
1st row (RS) [P1, K2] (9)10(11) times, (P1, K1)P1(0).
2nd row (K1, P1)P1(0), [P1, K1, P1] (9)10(11) times.
Cont in this way moving the P sts one st to the left on RS rows and one st to the right on WS rows, inc 1 st at each end of every foll 10th row until there are (37)39(41) sts.
Now work straight until sleeve measures (42)43(44)cm from top of rib ending with a WS row.
Cast off.

LEFT SLEEVE
Work as given for right sleeve to **.
Change to 7mm needles and cont in patt as given for back, but rep instructions in square brackets (9)10(11) times, instead of (19)20(21) times, and inc 1 st at each end of every foll 10th row until there are (41)43(45) sts.
Work straight until sleeve measures (42)43(44)cm from top of rib, ending with a WS row.
Cast off.

MAKING UP
Join the shoulder seams to (13)14(15)cm in from armhole edge to allow for a neck opening.
Join side and sleeve seams.
Set in sleeves.
Fold cuffs on to right side.

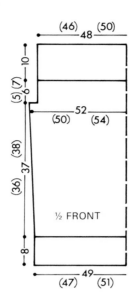

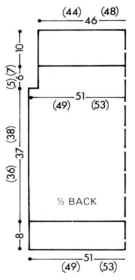

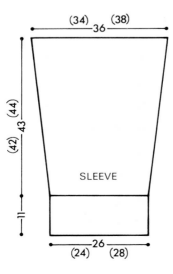

Photograph: A. Carrara   Designed by Sophie Serret

Mohair Seed Stitch

A multi-coloured seed-stitch pattern using vivid spots of colour on the dark background of a plain mohair sweater.

SIZES
To fit (86)91(96)cm bust

MATERIALS
(400)450(500)g mohair in main colour (A)
100g in 1st contrast colour (B)
50g each in 2nd, 3rd and 4th contrast colours (C, D, E)
1 pair each 3¾mm and 4½mm needles

TENSION
17 sts and 20 rows to 10cm over patt on 4½mm needles.

FRONT
Using 3¾mm needles and A, cast on (77)81(85) sts.
Work 5cm K1, P1 rib, inc 10 sts evenly over last row. (87)91(95) sts.
Change to 4½mm needles and commence patt from chart:
1st row (RS) K(1B)0(1A, 1B), *1A, 1B, 3A, 1B; rep from * to last (2)1(3) sts, K(1A, 1B)1A(1A, 1B, 1A).
2nd row P(1A, 1C)1C(2A, 1C), *5A, 1C; rep from * to last (1)0(2) sts, P(1A)0(2A).
3rd row K all the A sts, P all the C sts.
4th row P(1B, 1A)1A, (1A, 1B, 1A), *1B, 3A, 1B, 1A; rep from * to last (1)0(2) sts, P(1B)0(1B, 1A).
Work 4 rows st st in A.
These 8 rows establish the chart patt. Cont in patt working from chart. When chart is complete rep 1st–48th rows until front measures (38)39(40)cm from top of rib, ending with a WS row.
Shape armholes
Cast off 4 sts at beg of next 2 rows, then 2 sts at beg of foll 4 rows. Now dec 1 st at each end of next 2 rows (67)71(75) sts.**
Work straight until front measures (55)57(59)cm from top of rib, ending with a WS row.
Divide for neck
Next row Patt (23)25(27) sts, turn, leaving rem sts on a spare needle, cont on these sts only for left side of neck.
***Cast off 3 sts at neck edge on next row, then dec 1 st at neck edge on foll 2 alt rows. (18)20(22) sts.
Work straight until armhole measures (25)26(27)cm from beg, ending at armhole edge.
Shape shoulder
Cast off (9)10(11) sts at beg of next row.
Work 1 row. Cast off.
Return to sts on spare needle, with RS of work facing, rejoin yarn to next st.
Next row Cast off 21 sts, patt to end. (23)25(27) sts.
Work 1 row.
Complete to match left side of neck working from *** to end.

BACK
Work as given for front to **
Now work straight until back measures 2 rows less than front to shoulder, ending with a WS row.
Divide for neck
Next row Patt (23)25(27) sts, turn, leaving rem sts on a spare needle, cont on these sts only for right side of neck.
****Cast off 5 sts at beg of next row. (18)20(22) sts.
Shape shoulder
Cast off (9)10(11) sts at beg of next row.
Work 1 row.
Cast off.
Return to sts on spare needle, with RS of work facing rejoin yarn to next st, cast off 21 sts, patt to end. (23)25(27) sts.
Work 1 row. Complete to match right side of neck working from **** to end.

SLEEVES
Using 3¾mm needles and A, cast on (37)41(45) sts.
Work 5cm K1, P1 rib, inc (4)6(8) sts evenly across last row. (41)47(53) sts.
Change to 4½mm needles and cont in patt as set for 3rd size of front, inc 1 st at each end of every foll (7th)8th(9th) row until there are (61)65(69) sts. Work straight until sleeve measures (38)39(40)cm from top of rib, ending with a WS row.
Shape top
Cast off (3)4(5) sts at beg of next 2 rows.
Cast off 2 sts at beg of next 2 rows, then dec 1 st at each end of foll alt row. Rep from * to * 4 times more.
Now dec 1 st at each end of foll (7)8(9) alt rows. Cast off 2 sts at beg of next 2 rows.
Cast off rem 7 sts.

MAKING UP
Join right shoulder seam.
Neckband
Using 3¾mm needles and A, with RS of work facing, K up 101 sts around neck edge. Work 4cm K1, P1 rib. Cast off in rib.
Join left shoulder and neckband seams.
Join side and sleeve seams.
Set in sleeves.

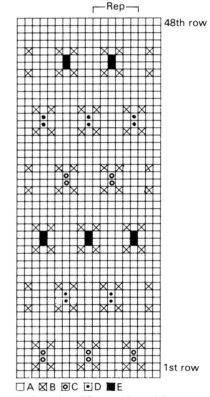

┌─Rep─┐
48th row

1st row

□A ⊠B ◙C ⊡D ■E

A, B — K on RS rows, P on WS rows
C, D, E — P on RS and WS rows

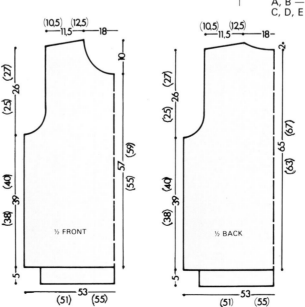

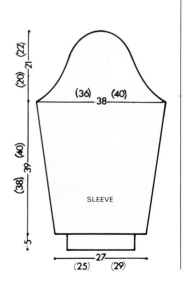

Photograph: G. Bensimon   Designed by Sophie Serret

Raglan Ribbed Dress

A slim raglan-sleeved sweater dress worked in fisherman's rib in four-ply yarn. Stylish and immensely wearable.

SIZES
To fit (81)86(91)cm bust

MATERIALS
(800)850(900)g four-ply yarn
1 pair each 2¾mm and 3¼mm needles
1 set four double-pointed 2¾mm needles

TENSION
23 sts and 36 rows to 10cm over patt on 3¼mm needles.

FRONT
Using 3¼mm needles, cast on (113)117(121) sts.
Commence patt:
1st row (WS) K to end.
2nd row K1, *P1, K next st in row below; rep from * to last 2 sts, P1, K1.
These 2 rows form the patt rep.
Cont in patt until work measures (70)72(74)cm from cast-on edge, ending with a WS row.
Shape raglan armholes
***Next row** Patt 3 sts, K3 tog, patt to last 6 sts, sl 1, K2 tog, psso, patt to end.
Patt 3 rows.***
Rep last 4 rows (14)15(16) times more, then 1st row again. 49 sts.
Patt 1 row.
Divide for neck
Next row Patt 16, turn, leaving rem sts on a spare needle.
Next row Cast off 3 sts, patt to end of row. 13 sts.
Now dec for raglan as before on next and 2 foll 4th rows, *at the same time* cast off 2 sts at neck edge on foll 3 alt rows.
Fasten off.
Return to sts on spare needle, with RS of work facing rejoin yarn to next st.
Next row Cast off 17 sts, patt to end of row. 16 sts.
Work 1 row.
Now cont to dec for raglan as before on next and 2 foll 4th rows, *at the same time* cast off 3 sts at neck edge on next row and 2 sts on foll 3 alt rows.
Fasten off.

BACK
Work as given for front to ***.
Rep last 4 rows (17)18(19) times more, then 1st row again. 37 sts.
Work 1 row.
Cast off.

SLEEVES
Using 2¾mm needles, cast on (57)61(65) sts.
Work 6cm K1, P1 rib.
Change to 3¼mm needles and cont in patt as given for front, inc 1 at each end of every 4th row until there are (87)91(95) sts.

Work straight until sleeve measures (32)33(34)cm from top of rib.
Shape raglan
Work as given for front of dress from ** to ***.
Rep last 4 rows (17)18(19) times more, then 1st row again. 11 sts.
Work 1 row.
Cast off.

MAKING UP
Join raglan seams.
Neckband
Using double-pointed 2¾mm needles, with RS of work facing, K up 100 sts around neck edge, beg at left back raglan seam. Work 2cm K1, P1 rib in rounds.
Cast off in rib.
Join side and sleeve seams.

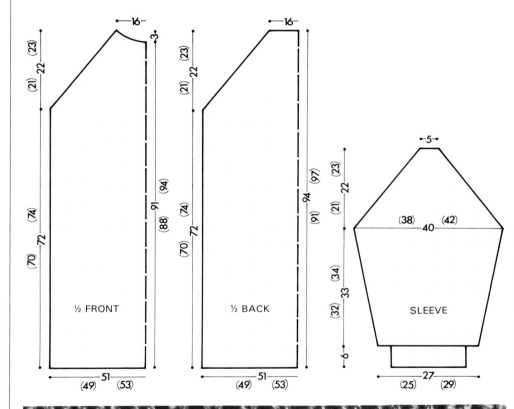

Chequers

Worked in a lightweight Icelandic-type wool equivalent to double knitting, this sweater has an interesting buttoned stand-up collar set into a V-shaped neck.

SIZES
To fit (81)86(91)cm bust

MATERIALS
(500)550(600)g double knitting yarn
1 pair each 2¾mm and 3¾mm needles
2 buttons

TENSION
22 sts and 28 rows to 10cm over patt on 3¾mm needles.

FRONT
Using 2¾mm needles, cast on (103)107(111) sts. Work 8cm K1, P1 rib. Change to 3¾mm needles and commence patt:
1st row (RS) P(1)3(5), K1, *P9, K1; rep from * to last (1)3(5) sts, P to end.
2nd and every alt row K(1)3(5), P1, *K9, P1; rep from * to last (1)3(5) sts, K to end.
3rd, 5th, 7th, 9th and 11th rows As 1st row.
13th row K to end.
14th row P to end.
These 14 rows form the patt rep.
Cont in patt until work measures (35)36(37)cm from top of rib ending with a WS row.
Shape armholes
Cast off 4 sts at beg of next 2 rows and 2 sts at beg of foll 4 rows. Now dec 1 st at each end of next and foll (1)2(3) alt rows. (83)85(87) sts.
Work straight until front measures (43)44(45)cm from top of rib ending with a WS row.
Divide for neck
Next row Patt (41)42(43), turn, leaving rem sts on a spare needle, cont on these sts only for left side of neck.
Shape neck
** Dec 1 st at neck edge on next and every foll alt row until (24)25(26) sts rem, ending at armhole edge.
Shape shoulder
Cast off 5 sts at beg of next and foll 3 alt rows. Work 1 row.
Cast off rem (4)5(6) sts.
Return to sts on spare needle. With RS of work facing, rejoin yarn to next st.
Next row Cast off 1 st, patt to end. (41)42(43) sts.
Complete right side of neck to match left side, working from ** to end.

BACK
Using 2¾mm needles, cast on (101)105(109) sts. Work 8cm K1, P1 rib. Change to 3¾mm needles and cont in patt.
1st row (RS) P(0)2(4), K1, *P9, K1; rep from * to last (0)2(4) sts, P(0)2(4).

2nd and every alt row K(0)2(4), P1, *K9, P1; rep from * to last (0)2(4) sts, K(0)2(4).
3rd, 5th, 7th, 9th and 11th rows As given for 1st row.
13th row K to end.
14th row P to end.
These 14 rows form the patt rep.
Cont in patt until work measures (35)36(37)cm from top of rib, ending with a WS row.
Shape armholes
Cast off 3 sts at beg of next 2 rows and 2 sts at beg of next 4 rows. Now dec 1 st at each end of next and foll (1)2(3) alt rows. (83)85(87) sts.
Work straight until back measures 2 rows less than front to shoulder, ending with a WS row.
Divide for neck
Next row Patt (31)32(33), turn, leaving rem sts on a spare needle and cont on these sts only for right side of neck.
Next row Work 2 tog, patt to end.
Shape shoulder
***Cast off 5 sts at beg of next and foll 3 alt rows, *at the same time* dec 1 st at neck edge on foll 6 rows.
Work 1 row.
Cast off rem (4)5(6) sts.
Return to sts on spare needle. With RS of work facing rejoin yarn to next st, cast off 22 sts, patt to end. (30)31(32) sts.
Now complete to match right side of neck working from *** to end.

LEFT SLEEVE
Using 2¾mm needles, cast on (57)59(61) sts. Work 8cm K1, P1 rib, inc (12)14(16) sts evenly across last row. (69)73(77) sts.
Change to 3¾mm needles and cont in patt:
1st row P(4)6(8), K1, *P9, K1; rep from * to last (4)6(8) sts, P to end.
2nd row K(4)6(8), P1, *K9, P1; rep from *

to last (4)6(8) sts, K to end.
3rd-14th rows Patt as given for 3rd-14th rows of front.
These 14 rows form the patt rep.
Cont in patt inc 1 st at each end of next and every foll 14th row until there are (81)85(89) sts.****
Work straight until sleeve measures 35cm from top of rib, ending with a WS row.
Shape top
Cast off 2 sts at beg of next row and 4 sts at beg of foll row. Now cast off 2 sts at beg of foll 6 rows. Dec 1 st at beg of next row. Cast off 2 sts at beg of next row. Now dec 1 st at beg of foll (14)18(22) rows. 46 sts. Now cast off 2 sts at beg of foll 12 rows and 4 sts at beg of foll 2 rows.
Cast off rem 14 sts.

RIGHT SLEEVE
Work as given for left sleeve to ****.
Work straight until sleeve measures 35cm from top of rib, ending with a RS row.
Shape top as given for left sleeve.

COLLAR
Using 2¾mm needles, cast on 127 sts.
Work in K1, P1 rib for 2cm.
1st buttonhole row Rib 4, cast off 3 sts, rib to end.
2nd buttonhole row Rib to end, casting on 3 sts over those cast off in previous row.
Cont in rib until work measures 7cm, ending at buttonhole edge.
Next row Rib 39, turn, leaving rem sts on spare needle.
*****Cast off 3 sts at beg of next and foll 2 alt rows, then 4 sts at beg of foll 6 alt rows, and 2 sts at beg of foll 3 alt rows, *at the same time* when work measures 9cm, ending at buttonhole edge, rep 1st–2nd buttonhole rows. When shaping is complete, fasten off.
Return to sts on spare needle. Rejoin yarn to inner edge, cast off 49 sts, rib to end.
Next row Rib to end.
Complete to match other side of collar from ***** to end omitting buttonhole.

Photograph: Sepp   Designed by Yolaine de Muynck

MAKING UP

Join shoulder, side and sleeve seams.
Set in sleeves.
Join on collar overlapping right edge over
left edge.
Sew on buttons.

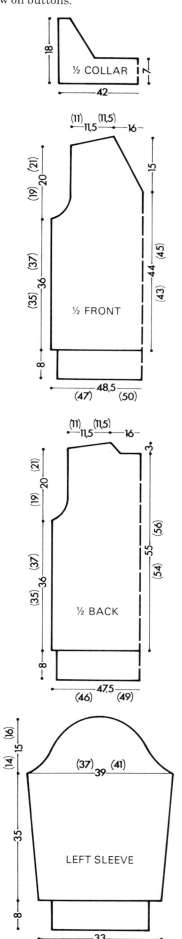

½ COLLAR

18

7

42

½ FRONT

(11) (11,5)
11,5 — 16

(21)
20
(19)

15

(37)
36
(35)

44 (45)
(43)

8

48,5
(47) (50)

½ BACK

(11) (11,5)
11,5 — 16

(21)
20
(19)

3

(37)
36
(35)

55 (56)
(54)

8

47,5
(46) (49)

LEFT SLEEVE

(16)
15
(14)

(37) (41)
39

35

8

33
(31) (35)

53

Chevron Pullover

A practical all-weather style that can be made as here in a soft wool and mohair mixture or in cotton for a cool summer top.

AUTUMN
★

SIZES
To fit (81)86(91)cm bust

MATERIALS
(500)550(550)g chunky yarn
1 pair each 5mm and 7mm needles

TENSION
10 sts and 16 rows to 10cm over patt on 7mm needles.

FRONT
Using 5mm needles, cast on (53)55(57) sts.
Work 9cm K1, P1 rib, inc 6 sts evenly across last row. (59)61(63) sts.
Change to 7mm needles and commence patt:
1st row (RS) P(0)1(2), [K2, P2] 7 times, K3, [P2, K2] 7 times, P(0)1(2).
2nd row (0)P1(K1, P1), [P1, K2, P1] 7 times, P1, K1, P1, [P1, K2, P1] 7 times, (0)P1(P1, K1).
3rd row K(0)1(2), [P2, K2] 7 times, P3, [K2, P2] 7 times, K(0)1(2).
4th row (0)K1(P1, K1), [K1, P2, K1] 7 times, K1, P1, K1, [K1, P2, K1] 7 times, (0)K1(K1, P1).
These 4 rows form the patt rep.
Cont in patt until front measures (33)34(35)cm from top of rib, ending with a WS row.
Divide for neck
Next row Patt (29)30(31) sts, turn, leaving rem sts on a spare needle, cont on these sts only for left side of neck.
****Dec 1 st at neck edge on next and foll 5 alt rows, ending at armhole edge. (23)24(25) sts.
Shape armhole
Cast off 3 sts at beg of next row and 2 sts at beg of foll alt row. (18)19(20) sts.
Now dec 1 st at neck edge on next and every foll 4th row until (12)13(14) sts rem.
Now work straight until armhole measures (17)18(19)cm from beg, ending at armhole edge.
Shape shoulder
Cast off (6)7(8) sts at beg of next row.
Work 1 row.
Cast off.
Return to sts on spare needle, with RS of work facing rejoin yarn to next st.
Next row Cast off 1 st, patt to end. (29)30(31) sts.
Complete to match left side of neck working from ** to end.

BACK
Using 5mm needles, cast on (45)47(49) sts.
Work 9cm K1, P1 rib, inc 6 sts evenly across last row. (51)53(55) sts.
Change to 7mm needles and work in patt as given for front, but working the instructions in square brackets 6 times instead of 7, until work matches front to armhole, ending with a WS row.
Shape armholes
Cast off 1 st at beg of next 2 rows. (49)51(53) sts. Work straight until back measures (53)55(57)cm from top of rib, ending with a WS row.
Divide for neck
Next row Patt (12)13(14) sts, turn, leaving rem sts on a spare needle, cont on these sts only for right side of neck.
***Work straight until armhole measures (16)17(18)cm from beg, ending at armhole edge.
Shape shoulder
Cast off (6)7(8) sts at beg of next row.
Work 1 row.
Cast off.
Return to sts on spare needle, with RS of work facing rejoin yarn to next st.
Next row Cast off 25 sts, patt to end. (12)13(14) sts.
Now complete to match right side of neck, working from *** to end.

MAKING UP
Join shoulder seams.
Armbands
Using 5mm needles, with RS of work facing, K up (48)52(56) sts.
Work 2cm K1, P1 rib.
Cast off loosely in rib.
Join side seams.
Neckband
Using 5mm needles, with RS of work facing, K up (53)56(57) sts between centre of back neck and point of 'V'.
Work 2cm K1, P1 rib.
Cast off loosely in rib.
Work a similar band on RH side of neck opening.
Join neckband seam at back neck.
Overlap LH edge of band at front over RH edge and stitch down.

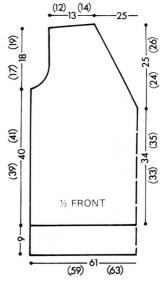

½ FRONT

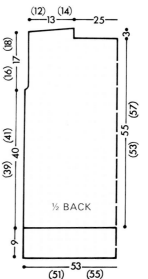

½ BACK

Photograph: J.-C. Benoit   Designed by Sophie Serret

Longline

A slinky ribbed cardigan with sewn-on patch pockets. Tricky to knit because of the shaping.

AUTUMN
★ ★ ★

SIZES
To fit 81–86(91–96)cm bust

MATERIALS
1400(1450)g Aran-weight yarn
1 pair each 4mm and 4½mm needles
5 buttons

TENSION
26 sts and 30 rows to 10cm over rib patt on 4½mm needles.

RIGHT FRONT
Using 4mm needles, cast on 69(73) sts.
Work 3cm K1, P1 rib. Change to 4½mm needles and commence rib patt:
1st row (RS) P2, *K1, P3; rep from * to last 3 sts, K1, P2.
2nd row K1, *P3, K1; rep from * to end.
These 2 rows form the patt rep.
Cont in patt until work measures 41(43)cm from top of rib, ending with a WS row.
Shape front neck and raglan
****Next row** Patt 4 sts, K2 tog, patt to last 6 sts, sl 1, K1, psso, patt to end.
Next row Patt to end.
Next row Patt to last 6 sts, sl 1, K1, psso, patt to end.
Next row Patt to end.
Next row Patt 4 sts, K2 tog, patt to last 6 sts, sl 1, K1, psso, patt to end.
Next row Patt to end.**
Rep from ** to ** once more.
Next row Patt 4 sts, K2 tog, patt to last 7 sts, sl 1, K2 tog, psso, patt to end.
Next row Patt to end.
Next row Patt to last 6 sts, sl 1, K1, psso, patt to end.
Next row Patt to end.
Cont in this way dec 1 st at neck edge on next row and foll 2nd and 4th rows alternately until 24(25) decs have been made at neck edge, *at the same time* dec 1 st at raglan edge on next and foll 4 alt rows, [dec 2 sts at raglan edge on next alt row, and 1 st on foll 6 alt rows] 3 times.
Now dec 1 st at raglan edge as before on foll 3(5) alt rows. Cast off rem 5 sts.

LEFT FRONT
Work as given for right front reversing all shapings, and replacing 'sl 1, K1, psso' and 'sl 1, K2 tog, psso' on raglan edge with 'K2 tog' and 'K3 tog', and 'K2 tog' on neck edge with 'sl 1, K1, psso'.

BACK
Using 4mm needles, cast on 141(149) sts.
Work 3cm K1, P1 rib.
Change to 4½mm needles and cont in rib patt as given for right front until work measures 41(43)cm from top of K1, P1 rib, ending with a WS row.

Shape raglans
*****Next row** Patt 4 sts, K2 tog, patt to last 6 sts, sl 1, K1, psso, patt to end.
Next row Patt to end.****
Rep from *** to *** 5 times more.
*******Next row** Patt 4 sts, K3 tog, patt to last 7 sts, sl 1, K2 tog, psso, patt to end.
Next row Patt to end.******
Rep from *** to ****** 4 times more.
61(69) sts.
Rep from *** to **** twice.
Rep from **** to ****** once.
2nd size only
Rep from *** to **** twice.
Rep from **** to ****** once.
Both sizes
Rep from *** to **** once more.
Cast off rem 51 sts.

RIGHT SLEEVE
Using 4mm needles cast on 57(65) sts.
Work 7cm K1, P1 rib.
Change to 4½mm needles and cont in rib patt as given for right front, inc 1 st at each end of every 3rd row until there are 113(121) sts.
Work straight until sleeve measures 37(38)cm from top of rib, ending with a WS row.
Shape top
Work as given for back from *** to **** 4 times.
Now work from *** to *** twice and from **** to **** once.
Rep last 6 rows 1(2) times more.
Rep from *** to *** twice more.
Next row Cast off 6 sts, patt to last 7 sts, sl 1, K2 tog, psso, patt to end.
Next row Patt to end.
Rep last 2 rows twice more.
Cast off rem 5 sts.

POCKETS (make 2)
Using 4½mm needles, cast on 41 sts.
Work in rib patt as given for right front until work measures 11cm.
Change to 4mm needles and work 2cm K1, P1 rib. Cast off loosely in rib.

FRONT AND NECK BORDER
Using 4mm needles, cast on 13 sts.
Work 4cm K1, P1 rib.
Make buttonhole:
1st buttonhole row Rib 5, cast off 3 sts, rib to end.
2nd buttonhole row Rib to end, casting on 3 sts over those cast off in previous row.
Cont in rib, making 4 more buttonholes at 9.5(10)cm intervals.
Cont in rib until band when slightly stretched fits up right front, round back neck and down left front.
Cast off in rib.

MAKING UP
Join raglan seams.
Join side and sleeve seams. Sew on front border, joining buttonhole section to right front.
Sew a pocket on to each front 8cm in from front borders and just above lower rib.
Sew on buttons.

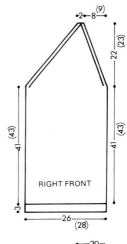

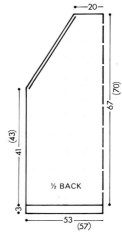

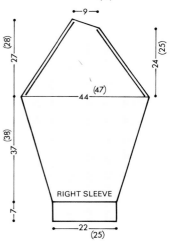

Photograph: J-L. de Sauverzac   Designed by Grand Confort

Carnival

**Vivid colours in spots and stripes
make a simple cardigan special.
It also has two knitted-in pockets.**

AUTUMN
★ ★

SIZES
To fit (4)6(8) years

MATERIALS
(250)250(300)g double knitting yarn in
main colour (A)
50g in each of 3 contrast colours (B, C, D)
1 pair each 3mm and 3¾mm needles.
5 buttons.

TENSION
24 sts and 29 rows to 10cm over st st on
3¾mm needles.

BACK
Using 3mm needles and A, cast on
(59)65(71) sts.
Work 5.5cm K1, P1 rib, inc 10 sts evenly
across last row. (69)75(81) sts.
Change to 3¾mm needles and cont in st st
until work measures (23)25(27)cm from
top of rib, ending with a WS row.
Shape armholes
Cast off 2 sts at beg of next 6 rows.
(57)63(69) sts.
Commence yoke patt:
K 2 rows in B, K 2 rows in A. Cont in st st
working 6 rows in jacquard patt from
chart 1.
K 2 rows in C, K 2 rows in D.
Cont in st st working 12 rows in jacquard
patt from chart 2.
K 2 rows in D, K 2 rows in C.
Work 2 rows st st in A, beg with a K row,
then cont in st st working 6 rows in
jacquard patt from chart 1.
K 2 rows in A, K 2 rows in B, *at the
same time* when work measures
(34.5)37.5(40.5)cm from top of rib, ending
with a WS row, divide for neck thus:
Next row Patt (14)17(20) sts, turn,
leaving rem sts on a spare needle, cont
on these sts only for right side of neck.
Work 1 row.
Cast off.
Return to sts on spare needle, with RS of
work facing rejoin yarn to next st, cast off
29 sts, patt to end. (14)17(20) sts.
Work 2 rows.
Cast off.

POCKET LININGS (make 2)
Using 3¾mm needles and A, cast on 23
sts. Work 6cm st st, ending with a P row.
Leave these sts on a st holder.

RIGHT FRONT
Using 3mm needles and A, cast on
(32)35(38) sts.
Work 5.5cm K1, P1 rib, inc 5 sts evenly
across last row. (37)40(43) sts.
Change to 3¾mm needles and work in st
st until front measures 6cm from top of
rib, ending with a WS row.

Place pocket
Next row K9, sl next 23 sts on a st holder,
K across sts on pocket lining st holder,
K to end of row.
Cont in st st until work measures
(23)25(27)cm from top of rib, ending with
a RS row.
Shape armhole
Cast off 2 sts at beg of next and foll 2 alt
rows. (31)34(37) sts.
Now cont in yoke patt as given for back
until work measures (28)31(34)cm from
top of rib, ending with a WS row.
Shape neck
Cast off 7 sts at beg of next row, 4 sts at
beg of foll alt row, then 3 sts at beg of next
alt row. Now dec 1 st at beg of 3 foll alt
rows. (14)17(20) sts.
Work straight until front measures same
as back to cast-off row, ending with a RS
row.
Cast off.

LEFT FRONT
Work as given for right front, reversing
pocket placing, all shapings and direction
of zigzag on jacquard patt from chart 2.

SLEEVES
Using 3mm needles and A, cast on
(41)47(53) sts.
Work 5.5cm K1, P1 rib, inc 6 sts evenly
across last row. (47)53(59) sts.
Change to 3¾mm needles and cont in st
st, inc 1 st at each end of every foll 6th row
until there are (63)69(75) sts.
Work straight until sleeve measures
(25)28(31)cm from top of rib, ending with
a WS row.

Shape top
K 2 rows B, K 2 rows A, work 2 rows
jacquard patt from chart 1, *at the same
time* cast off 2 sts at beg of each row.
(51)57(63) sts.
Work rem 4 rows jacquard patt from
chart 1.
K 2 rows C, K 2 rows D.
Cast off.

MAKING UP
Join shoulder seams and side seams.
Join sleeve seams. Set in sleeves.
Neckband
Using 3mm needles and A, with WS of
work facing, P up 85 sts around neck edge.
K 1 row tbl. Work 2.5cm K1, P1 rib. Cast
off in rib.
Left front band
Using 3mm needles and A, with WS of
work facing, P up (100)108(116) sts along
left front edge and neck border.
K 1 row tbl.
Work 1.5cm K1, P1 rib, ending with a WS
row.
1st buttonhole row Rib 5, cast off 2 sts,
[rib (20)22(24) including st used to cast
off, cast off 2 sts] 4 times, rib to end.
2nd buttonhole row Rib to end, casting
on sts over those cast off in previous
row.
Cont in rib until band measures 3cm from
beg. Cast off in rib.
Right front band
Work as given for left front band, omitting
buttonholes.
Sew down pocket linings and pocket
edgings.
Sew on buttons.

Chart 1

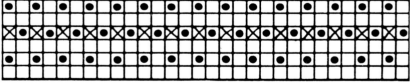

1st row

Chart 2

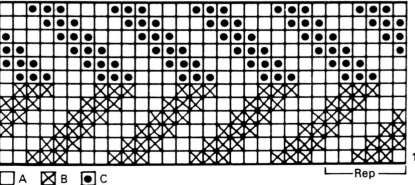

1st row

☐ A ☒ B ⊡ C

Rep

Photograph: J.-P. Decros Designed by Dany Ribaillier

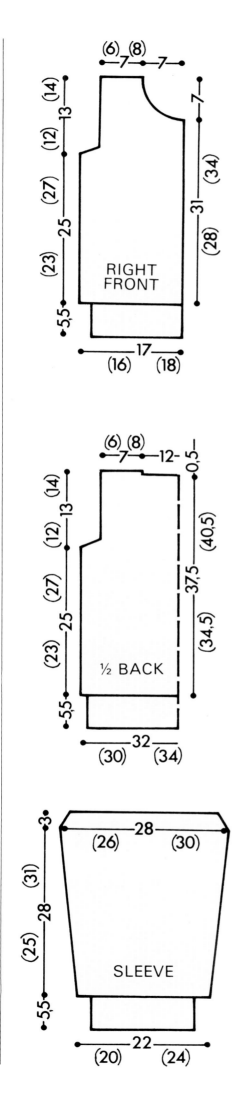

RIGHT FRONT

(6) (8)
7 — 7

(14)
13

(12)

(27)
25

(23)

5,5

17
(16) (18)

7
(34)
31
(28)

½ BACK

(6) (8)
7 — 12 — 0,5

(14)
13

(12)

(27)
25

(23)

5,5

32
(30) (34)

(40,5)
37,5
(34,5)

SLEEVE

3
28
(26) (30)

(31)
28
(25)

5,5

22
(20) (24)

Chunky Gilet

Soft natural Icelandic wool has been used for a boxy ribbed gilet that could hardly be easier or quicker to knit.

SIZES
To fit (81)86(91)cm bust

MATERIALS
(400)450(450)g chunky yarn
1 pair each 3¾mm and 6mm needles

TENSION
12 sts and 20 rows to 10cm over patt on 6mm needles.

RIGHT FRONT
Using 6mm needles, cast on (33)35(37) sts.
Commence patt:
1st row [K2, P2] to last (1)3(1) sts, (K1) K2, P1(K1).
This row forms the patt rep.
Cont in patt until work measures (42)44(46)cm.
Shape neck
Cast off 5 sts at beg of next row, 4 sts at beg of foll alt row, 3 sts at beg of foll alt row, then 2 sts at beg of foll alt row.
Now dec 1 st at beg of foll 2 alt rows.
(17)19(21) sts.
Work straight until right front measures (52)54(56)cm from cast-on edge.
Cast off.

LEFT FRONT
Work as given for right front, working 1 row less before neck shaping.

BACK
Using 6mm needles, cast on (53)57(61) sts.
Work in patt as given for 1st size of right front until work measures (47)49(51)cm from cast-on edge.
Shape neck
Next row Patt (22)24(26), turn, leaving rem sts on a spare needle, cont on these sts only for first side of neck.
**Cast off 3 sts at beg of next row and 2 sts at beg of foll alt row. (17)19(21) sts.
Now work straight until back measures (50)52(54)cm from beg.
Cast off.
Return to sts on spare needle, rejoin yarn to inner end.
Next row Cast off 9 sts, patt to end. (22)24(26) sts.
Work 1 row.
Complete to match first side of neck from ** to end.

MAKING UP
Join shoulder seams.
Neckband
Using 3¾mm needles, with RS of work facing, K up (76)78(80) sts around neck edge.
Work 2cm K2, P2 rib. Cast off in rib.
Armbands
Mark armholes (30)31(32)cm from cast-on

edge on back and fronts.
Using 3¾mm needles, with RS of work facing, K up (76)80(84) sts around armhole edge.
Work 2cm K2, P2 rib. Cast off in rib.

Join side seams.
Make 4 plaited cords each one 22cm long.
On each front attach one cord to neck edge just below neckband and another 14cm below that.

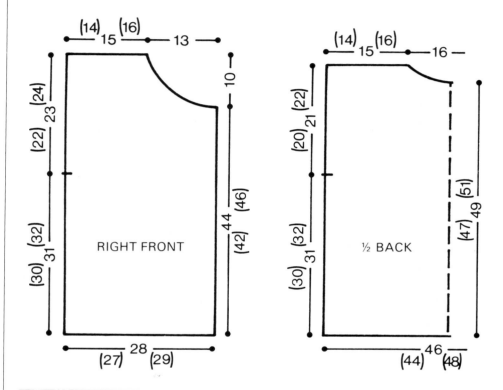

Photograph: J.-P. Metayer   Designed by Jacqueline Boiffils for Le Printemps

Parisian

A beautiful zip-up jacket with raglan sleeves and padded shoulders in an unusual rib.

SIZES
To fit (81)86(91)cm bust

MATERIALS
(1300)1400(1400)g double knitting yarn
1 pair each 3¼mm, 3¾mm and 4mm
needles
1 open-ended (62)64(66)cm zip
2 12cm zips
2 shoulder pads

TENSION
20 sts and 40 rows to 10cm over patt on
4mm needles.

RIGHT FRONT
Using 3¼mm needles, cast on (61)63(65)
sts. Work 7cm K1, P1 rib.
Change to 4mm needles and commence
rib patt:
1st row (RS) K to end, dec 5 sts evenly
across row. (56)58(60) sts.
2nd row *K1, K next st in row below; rep
from * to end.
Rep 2nd row only.
Cont in patt until work measures 13cm
from top of rib, ending with a WS row.
Place pocket opening
Next row (RS) Patt (18)20(22) sts, cast off
24 sts, patt 14 sts.
Next row Patt to end, casting on 24 sts
over those cast off in previous row.
Cont in patt until work measures
(34)35(36)cm from top of rib, ending with
a RS row.
Shape raglan armhole
Next row P3, patt to end.
Next row Patt to last 4 sts, K2 tog, K2.
Rep last 2 rows (27)29(31) times more, *at
the same time,* when 45 sts rem, ending
with a WS row, dec 1 st at neck edge on
next and every foll 4th row until 18 sts
rem.
Now cont to dec for neck on every foll 4th
row as set, dec 1 st for raglan on every foll
4th row instead of every alt row until 3 sts
rem.
Cast off.

LEFT FRONT
Work as given for right front, reversing
pocket placing and all shapings, working
sl 1, K1, psso instead of work 2 tog at
raglan edge.

BACK
Using 3¼mm needles, cast on
(122)126(130) sts.
Work 7cm K1, P1 rib.
Change to 4mm needles and K 1 row dec
12 sts evenly across row.
(110)114(118) sts.
Cont in 2nd row of patt as given for right

front until work measures (34)35(36)cm
from top of rib, ending with a WS row.
Shape raglan armholes
**Next row K2, sl 1, K1, psso, patt to last
4 sts, K2 tog, K2.
Next row P3, patt to last 3 sts, P3.**
Rep last 2 rows until 30 sts rem.
***Next row K2, sl 1, K1, psso, patt to
last 4 sts, K2 tog, K2.
Patt 3 rows.***
Rep last 4 rows until 22 sts rem, ending
with a dec row.
Cast off.

RIGHT SLEEVE
Using 3¼mm needles, cast on (48)52(56)
sts. Work 7cm K1, P1 rib.
Change to 4mm needles and K1 row, inc 8
sts evenly across row. (56)60(64) sts.
Cont in 2nd row of patt as given for right
front, inc 1 st at each end of every foll 8th
row until there are (92)96(100) sts.
Now work straight until work measures
(37)38(39)cm, ending with a WS row.
Shape top
Rep from ** to ** as given for back until
72 sts rem, then from *** to *** as given
for back 4 times. 64 sts.
Next row K2, sl 1, K1, psso, patt 26 sts,
sl 2 tog K-wise, K1, p2sso, patt to last 4
sts, K2 tog, K2. 60 sts.
Next row Patt 28 sts, P3, patt to end.
Next row Patt 29 sts, K3, patt to end.
Next row Patt 28 sts, P3, patt to end.
****Rep from *** to *** of back twice, but
cont to work st st over centre 3 sts. 56 sts.
Next row K2, sl 1, K1, psso, patt to centre
3 sts, sl 2 tog K-wise, p2sso, patt to last
4 sts, K2 tog, K2. 52 sts.
Patt 3 rows (do not work st st over centre 3
sts).****
Rep from *** to *** of back twice. 48 sts.
Next row K2, sl 1, K1, psso, patt 18 sts,
sl 2 tog K-wise, K1, p2sso, patt to last 4
sts, K2 tog, K2. 44 sts.
Next row Patt 20 sts, P3, patt to end.
Next row Patt 21 sts, K3, patt to,end.
Next row Patt 20 sts, P3, patt to end.
Rep from **** to ****.
Rep from *** to *** of back 3 times. 30 sts.
Next row Cast off 7 sts, patt to last 4 sts,
K2 tog, K2. 22 sts.
Next row Patt to end.
Next row Cast off 7 sts, patt to end. 15 sts.
Next row Patt to end.
Next row Cast off 7 sts, patt to last 4 sts,
K2 tog, K2.
Work 1 row.
Cast off rem 7 sts.

LEFT SLEEVE
Work as given for right sleeve until 30 sts
rem. Work 1 row.
Complete as given for right sleeve.

COLLAR
Using 3¾mm needles, cast on 3 sts.
Work in K1, P1 rib, inc 1 st at end of every
foll RS row until there are 23 sts, ending
with a RS row.
Now cast on 2 sts at beg of next and 2 foll
alt rows.
Work 1 row.
Cast on 5 sts at beg of next and foll alt row
and 6 sts at beg of next alt row.
Work 1 row.
Cast on (18)20(22) sts at the beg of the
next row. Leave these (63)65(67) sts on a
st holder.
Make a second piece the same way
reversing shaping by inc at beg of RS rows
instead of end. Now rib across both sets of
sts with straight edges at each side.
(126)130(134) sts.
Work 14cm K1, P1 rib, ending with a WS
row.
Next row Rib 45, turn, leaving rem sts on
spare needle cont on these sts only for
first side of collar.
Cast off 6 sts at beg of next row and 5 sts
at beg of 2 foll alt rows.
Cast off 2 sts at beg of 3 foll alt rows, then
dec 1 st at beg of every alt row until 3 sts
rem.
Cast off.
Return to sts on spare needle, with RS of
work facing rejoin yarn to inner edge, cast
off (36)40(44) sts, rib to end. 45 sts.
Rib 1 row.
Complete to match first side of collar
reversing shaping.

POCKET LININGS (make 2)
Using 3¾mm needles, cast on 30 sts.
Work 12cm st st.
Cast off.

Photograph: Turillazzi   Designed by Grand Confort

MAKING UP

Join raglan seams. Join side and underarm seams. Fold collar in half and join on to neck edge. Sew longest zip to front edges. Sew shorter zips to pocket openings. Sew in pocket linings. Sew in shoulder pads.

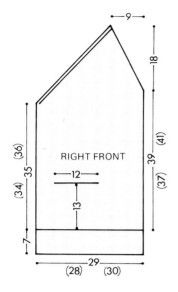

RIGHT FRONT

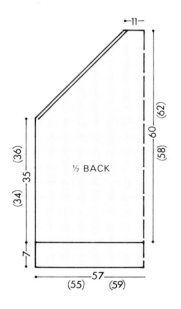

½ BACK

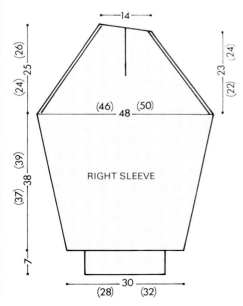

RIGHT SLEEVE

Preppy

A shawl-collared classic is given some distinction with bands of triangles in natural alpaca shades worked on the body and sleeves.

AUTUMN ★ ★

SIZES
To fit (96)101(106)cm chest

MATERIALS
(400)450(450)g Aran-weight yarn in main colour (A)
100g in 1st contrast colour (B)
50g in each of 2nd and 3rd contrast colours (C, D)
1 pair each 4mm and 5mm needles.

TENSION
19 sts and 22 rows to 10cm over st st on 5mm needles.

FRONT
Using 4mm needles and A, cast on (105)109(113) sts. Work 9cm K1, P1 rib.
Change to 5mm needles and cont in st st until work measures 12cm from top of rib, ending with a WS row. Break off A.
Commence triangle patt:
1st row (RS) K(8)10(12)B, *1C, 21B; rep from * to last (9)11(13) sts, 1C, K to end in B.
2nd and every alt row P to end, working B sts in B and C sts in C.
3rd row K(7)9(11)B, 1C, *2C, 19B, 1C; rep from * to last (9)11(13) sts, 2C, K to end in B.
5th row K(6)8(10)B, 2C, *3C, 17B, 2C; rep from * to last (9)11(13) sts, 3C, K to end in B.
7th row K(5)7(9)B, 3C, *4C, 15B, 3C; rep from * to last (9)11(13) sts, 4C, K to end in B.
9th row K(4)6(8)B, 4C, *5C, 13B, 4C; rep from * to last (9)11(13) sts, 5C, K to end in B.
11th row K(3)5(7)B, 5C, *6C, 11B, 5C; rep from * to last (9)11(13) sts, 6C, K to end in B.
13th row K(2)4(6)B, 6C, *7C, 9B, 6C; rep from * to last (9)11(13) sts, 7C, K to end in B.
15th row K(1)3(5)B, 7C, *8C, 7B, 7C; rep from * to last (9)11(13) sts, 8C, K to end in B.
17th row K(0)2(4)B, 8C, *9C, 5B, 8C; rep from * to last (9)11(13) sts, 9C, K to end in B.
19th row K(0)1(3)B, (8)9(9)C, *10C, 3B, 9C; rep from * to last (9)11(13) sts, (9)10(10) C, (0)1(3)B.
21st row K(8C)10B(1C, 10C), *11C, 1B, 10C; rep from * to last (9)11(13) sts, (9C)11C(11C, 1B, 1C).
22nd row As 2nd row.
These 22 rows form the triangle patt.
Rep the 22 rows once more using D instead of B, and B instead of C.**
Change to A and cont in st st until work measures (35)36(37)cm from top of rib, ending with a WS row.

Divide for neck
Next row K(32)34(36), turn, leaving rem sts on a spare needle, cont on these sts only for left side of neck.
Work straight until work measures (56)58(60)cm from top of rib, ending with a WS row.
Cast off.
Return to sts on spare needle, with RS of work facing, rejoin yarn to next st, cast off 41 sts, K to end. (32)34(36) sts.
Complete to match left side of neck.

BACK
Work as given for front to **.
Change to A and cont in st st until work measures (56)58(60)cm from top of rib, ending with a WS row.
Cast off.

SLEEVES
Using 4mm needles and A, cast on (47)51(55) sts.
Work 10cm K1, P1 rib.
Change to 5mm needles and work 26 rows st st, inc 1 st at each end of 1st and every foll 4th row. (61)65(69) sts.
Now work 1st–22nd rows of triangle patt as given for front, *at the same time* inc as before on every foll 3rd row.
Now change to A and cont in st st, inc as before until there are (91)95(99) sts.
Work straight until sleeve measures (39)40(41)cm, ending with a WS row.
Cast off.

COLLAR
Using 4mm needles and A, cast on (191)197(203) sts.
Work 22cm K1, P1 rib.
Cast off.

MAKING UP
Join shoulder seams. Set sleeves in flat matching centre of cast-off edge of sleeve to shoulder seam.
Join side and sleeve seams.
Join cast-on edge of collar to back and side of neck edge. Join row ends to front neck, crossing left side over right side.

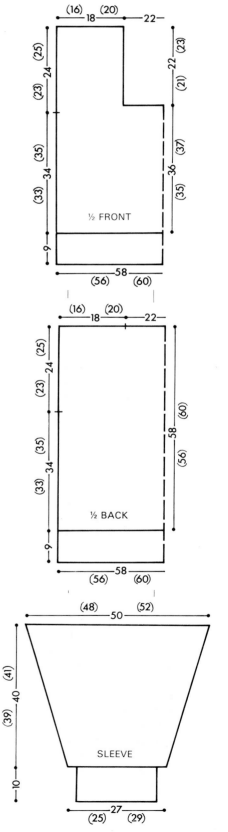

Photograph: J.-C. Benoit   Designed by Alain Piédelièvre

Cute Cable

Even budding tough guys must look smart sometimes. The cables are only on the front so it's not too daunting. This one is in cashmere, but it looks equally good in plain wool or synthetic yarns.

SIZES
To fit age (4)6(8) years

MATERIALS
(150)150(200)g double knitting yarn
1 pair each 3mm and 3¾mm needles
1 set four double-pointed 3mm needles
Cable needle

TENSION
22 sts and 30 rows to 10cm over st st on 3¾mm needles.

SPECIAL ABBREVIATIONS
Cable 6 back – sl next 3 sts on to cable needle and hold at back of work, K3, then K3 from cable needle.
Cable 6 front – sl next 3 sts on to cable needle and hold at front of work, K3, then K3 from cable needle.

FRONT
Using 3mm needles, cast on (84)90(96) sts. Work 3cm K1, P1 rib, inc 4 sts evenly across last row. (88)94(100) sts. Change to 3¾mm needles and commence patt:
1st row (RS) K(24)27(30), sl 1 P-wise, P2, K6, P2, ybk, sl 1 P-wise, P2, K12, P2, ybk, sl 1 P-wise, P2, K6, P2, ybk, sl 1 P-wise, K(24)27(30).
2nd and every alt row P(24)27(30), P1 tbl, K2, P6, K2, P1 tbl, K2, P12, K2, P1 tbl, K2, P6, K2, P1 tbl, P(24)27(30).
3rd row As 1st row.
5th row K(24)27(30), sl 1 P-wise, P2, cable 6 back, P2, ybk, sl 1 P-wise, P2, cable 6 back, cable 6 front, P2, ybk, sl 1 P-wise, P2, cable 6 back, P2, ybk, sl 1 P-wise, K(24)27(30).
7th row As 1st row.
9th row K(24)27(30), sl 1 P-wise, P2, cable 6 back, P2, ybk, sl 1 P-wise, P2, K12, P2, ybk, sl 1 P-wise, P2, cable 6 back, P2, ybk, sl 1 P-wise, K(24)27(30).
11th row K(24)27(30), sl 1 P-wise, P2, K6, P2, ybk, sl 1 P-wise, P2, cable 6 back, cable 6 front, P2, ybk, sl 1 P-wise, P2, K6, P2, ybk, sl 1 P-wise, K(24)27(30).

13th row As 9th row.
The 2nd-13th rows form the patt rep.
Cont in patt until work measures approx (18)20(22)cm from top of rib, ending with a 4th or 10th patt row.
Divide for neck
Next row Patt (44)47(50) sts, turn, leaving rem sts on a spare needle, cont on these sts only for left side of neck.
Shape armhole
**Dec 1 st at neck edge on next and every foll 4th row (8)9(10) times, *at the same time* cast off 5 sts at armhole edge on next alt row, then 3 sts on foll 2 alt rows, then 2 sts on next alt row and 1 st on foll alt row. (21)23(25) sts.
Now work straight until armhole measures (16)17(18)cm from beg, ending at armhole edge.
Shape shoulder
Cast off (7)8(9) sts at beg of next and foll alt row. 7 sts.
Work 1 row.
Cast off.
Return to sts on spare needle, with RS of work facing rejoin yarn to next st.
Complete to match left side of neck working from ** to end.

BACK
Using 3mm needles, cast on (80)86(92) sts. Work 3cm K1, P1 rib, inc 4 sts evenly across last row. (84)90(96) sts.
Change to 3¾mm needles and cont in st st until back measures same as front to armhole, ending with a P row.
Shape armholes
Cast off 5 sts at beg of next 2 rows, then 3 sts at beg of foll 4 rows and 2 sts at beg of foll 2 rows. Now dec 1 st at each end of next row. (56)62(68) sts.
Work straight until armhole measures (16)17(18)cm, ending with a P row.
Shape shoulders
Cast off (6)7(8) sts at beg of next 4 rows, then 6 sts at beg of foll 2 rows.
Work 1 row.
Cast off.

MAKING UP
Join shoulder seams.
Armbands
Using 3mm needles, with RS of work facing, K up (86)92(98) sts around armhole edge.
Work 4 rows K1, P1 rib.
Cast off loosely in rib.
Join side seams.
Neckband
Using double-pointed 3mm needles, with RS of work facing, K up (90)96(102) sts around neck edge.
Work 4 rounds K1, P1 rib making the st at centre of 'V' a K st and dec 1 st on each side of the centre st on every round.
Cast off loosely in rib.

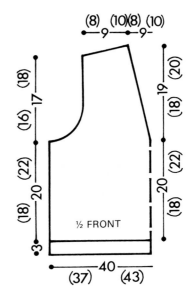

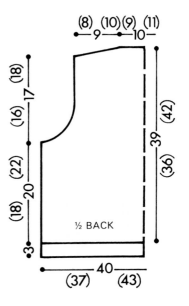

Photograph: M. Momy   Designed by Lil pour l'Autre

Tartan Chic

An elegant Chanel-style jacket with padded shoulders and knitted-in pockets. The contrast colours are also woven through the garter-stitch borders and used for knotted tassels.

SIZES
To fit 81–86cm bust

MATERIALS
600g Aran-weight yarn in main colour (A)
100g in each of 2 contrast colours (B, C)
1 pair 4½mm needles
2 shoulder pads

TENSION
18 sts and 26 rows to 10cm over st st on 4½mm needles.

POCKET LININGS (make 2)
Using A, cast on 24 sts.
Work 30 rows st st, ending with a WS row.
Leave sts on a st holder.

RIGHT FRONT
Using A, cast on 50 sts.
Commence patt:
1st row (RS) K5, *P1, K1, P1, K14; rep from *, ending last rep K8.
2nd row K all the P sts of previous row and P all the K sts.
These 2 rows form patt rep.
Rep the last 2 rows 12 times more.
Now rep 1st row using B, 2nd row using A, then 1st row using C, 2nd row using A.
Cont in patt in A, work 2 rows.
Place pocket
Next row Patt 22 sts, cast off 24 sts, patt across pocket lining sts, patt 4 sts. 50 sts.
Cont in patt, work 33 rows in A, 1 row in B, 1 row in A, 1 row in C, 4 rows in A. The last 40 rows form the colour sequence.
Cont in patt foll colour sequence as set until work measures 33cm from beg, ending with a RS row.
Shape armhole
Cast off 5 sts at beg of next row and 2 sts at beg of foll alt row, now dec 1 st at armhole edge on every alt row until there are 39 sts.
Work straight until front measures 50cm from beg, ending at neck edge.
Shape neck
Cast off 7 sts at beg of next row and 4 sts at beg of foll alt row, now dec 1 st at beg of foll 3 alt rows. 25 sts.
Work straight until armhole measures 23cm from beg, ending at armhole edge.
Shape shoulder
Cast off 8 sts at beg of next and foll alt row. Work 1 row.
Cast off.

LEFT FRONT
Work as given for right front, reversing patt, pocket placing and all shapings.

BACK
Using A, cast on 104 sts.
Commence patt:

1st row (RS) K8, *P1, K1, P1, K14; rep from * ending last rep K8.
2nd row K all the P sts of previous row and P all the K sts.
These 2 rows form patt rep.
Cont in patt working rows in same colour sequence as right front until back measures 33cm from beg, ending on same patt row as front to armhole.
Shape armholes
Cast off 5 sts at beg of next 2 rows, then 2 sts at beg of foll 2 rows. Now dec 1 st at each end of next and 3 foll alt rows. 82 sts.
Work straight until armhole measures 23cm from beg.
Shape shoulders
Cast off 8 sts at beg of next 4 rows and 9 sts at beg of foll 2 rows. Cast off rem 32 sts.

SLEEVES
Using A, cast on 51 sts.
Commence patt:
1st row (RS) K7, *P1, K1, P1, K14, rep from * ending last rep K7.
2nd row K all the P sts of previous row and P all the K sts.
These 2 rows form patt rep.
Working 1 row in B, 1 row in A, 1 row in C and 37 rows in A in sequence, inc 1 st at each end of every foll 8th row until there are 73 sts.
Work straight until sleeve measures 40cm from beg, ending on same patt row as right front to armhole.
Shape top
Cast off 3 sts at beg of next 2 rows, then 2 sts at beg of foll 2 rows, now dec 1 st at each end of every alt row until there are 31 sts. Cast off 3 sts at beg of next 4 rows. Cast off rem 19 sts.

FRONT, LOWER EDGE AND NECK BORDER,
Using A, cast on 5 sts.
Work 250cm g st. Cast off.

POCKET BORDERS
Using A cast on 5 sts.
Work 13cm g st. Cast off.

SLEEVE BORDERS
Using A, cast on 5 sts.
Work 28cm g st. Cast off.

MAKING UP
Work vertical lines of chain stitch on back, fronts and sleeves thus: work a line in C over the P sts to the right of each single K st on the RS of the work; work a line in B over the P sts to the left of each single K st.
Knot tassels in B and C alternately through the fabric where the lines of chain stitch cross the B and C rows.

Join shoulder seams and side seams.
Join sleeve seams and set in sleeves.
Sew down pocket linings. Join on pocket borders.
Join on front, neck and lower edge border beg and ending at back neck.
Join on sleeve borders.
Using 3 strands of yarn together, weave 1 row of B and 1 of C through all borders.
Sew in shoulder pads.

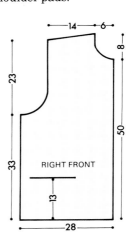

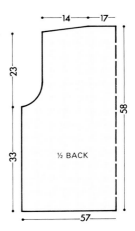

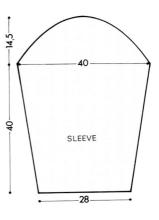

Photograph: Toscani   Designed by Jean-Paul Gaultier for Elle

Honeycomb

Raglan sweater worked in an interesting textured stitch pattern. It would look just as good in wool or cotton.

AUTUMN
★ ★

SIZES
To fit (81)86(91)cm bust

MATERIALS
(600)600(650)g double knitting yarn
1 pair each 3¼mm and 4mm needles
1 set four double-pointed 3¼mm needles

TENSION
26 sts and 32 rows to 10cm over patt on 4mm needles.

FRONT
Using 3¼mm needles, cast on (110)114(122) sts.
Work 7cm K2, P2 rib, inc 16 sts evenly over last row. (126)130(138) sts.
Change to 4mm needles and commence patt:
1st and 3rd rows (RS) K to end.
2nd row K1, *yrn, P2, pass yrn over 2 P sts and off needle, P2; rep from * to last st, K1.
4th row K1, *P2, yrn, P2, pass yrn over 2 P sts and off needle; rep from * to last st, K1.
These 4 rows form patt rep.
Cont in patt until work measures (31)32(33)cm from top of rib, ending with a WS row.
Shape raglans
Cast off (3)3(5) sts at beg of next 2 rows, then 2 sts at beg of next (8)10(12) rows. 104 sts.**
Now dec 1 st at each end of next and foll 27 alt rows, *at the same time*, when 66 sts rem, ending with a WS row, divide for neck thus: cast off the centre 20 sts and shape each side of neck separately by casting off 4 sts at neck edge on next row, then 3 sts on foll alt row and 2 sts on foll alt row, finally, dec 1 st at neck edge on next 5 alt rows. Fasten off.

BACK
Work as given for front to **.
Now dec 1 st at each end of next and foll 31 alt rows.
Cast off rem 40 sts.

RIGHT SLEEVE
Using 3¼mm needles, cast on (54)58(66) sts.
Work 7cm K2, P2 rib, inc 36 sts evenly across last row. (90)94(102) sts.
Change to 4mm needles and cont in patt as given for front, inc 1 st at each end of every foll 10th row until there are (106)110(118) sts.
Now work straight until sleeve measures (37)38(39)cm from top of rib, ending with a WS row.
Shape raglans
Cast off (3)3(5) sts at the beg of next 2 rows, then 2 sts at the beg of next (8)10(12) rows.
Now dec 1 st at each end of next and foll 27 alt rows, ending with a WS row.
Shape sleeve head
Cast off 6 sts at beg of next and foll 2 alt rows, *at the same time* dec 1 st at end of next and foll 2 alt rows.
Work 1 row.
Cast off rem 7 sts.

LEFT SLEEVE
Work as given for right sleeve reversing sleeve head shaping.

MAKING UP
Join raglan seams.
Join side and sleeve seams.
Neckband
Using four double-pointed 3¼mm needles, K up 124 sts around neck edge.
Work 2.5cm K2, P2 rib.
Cast off loosely in rib.

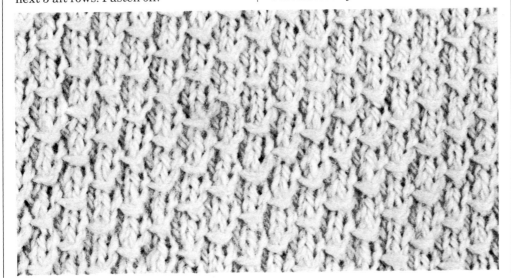

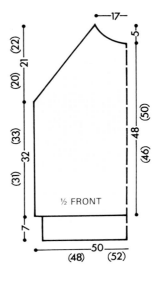

½ FRONT

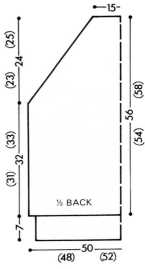

½ BACK

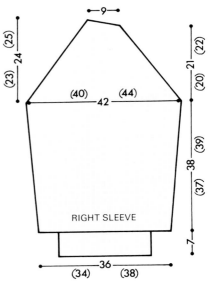

RIGHT SLEEVE

Photograph: J.-P. Decros Designed by Alain Derda for Pingouin

Stripey

A puff-sleeved cardigan with multicoloured patterned stripes neatly matched on the sleeves.

SIZES
To fit (81)86(91)cm bust

MATERIALS
(150)200(200)g double knitting yarn in main colour (A)
100g in each of 7 contrast colours (B, C, D, E, F, G, H)
1 pair each 3mm and 4mm needles
5 buttons

TENSION
22 sts and 28 rows to 10cm over patt on 4mm needles.

RIGHT FRONT
Using 3mm needles and A, cast on (38)40(42) sts.
Work 6cm K1, P1 rib, inc 11 sts evenly across last row. (49)51(53) sts.
Change to 4mm needles and commence patt from chart:
1st row (RS) With B, K to end.
2nd row With B, P to end.
3rd row K(0)1C,(1B, 1C), *2C, 5B, 1C; rep from * to last (1)2(3) sts, (1C)2C(2C, 1B).
4th row P(1C)1B, 1C(1C, 1B, 1C), *1B, 1C, 3B, 1C, 1B, 1C; rep from * to last (0)1(2) sts, (0)1B(1B, 1C).
These 4 rows set the position of the chart. Cont in patt from chart working the motif and background colours in the foll sequence: C on B, E on D, G on F, H on A, B on C, D on E, F on G, A on H (when sequence is complete return once more to C on B and so on). Work straight until front measures (19)20(21)cm from top of rib, ending with a WS row.
Shape front and armhole
Dec 1 st at neck edge on next and 5 foll alt rows, then on 10 foll 4th rows, *at the same time*, when (44)46(48) sts rem, ending at side edge, cast off 5 sts at beg of next row, then cast off 3 sts at beg of foll alt row, 2 sts at beg of next alt row and 1 st at beg of foll alt row, then inc 1 st at armhole edge on 2 foll 8th rows. (24)26(28) sts.
Work (3)5(7) rows straight.
Shape shoulder
Cast off 8 sts at beg of next row, then (8)9(10) sts at beg of foll alt row.
Work 1 row.
Cast off.

LEFT FRONT
Work as given for right front reversing all shapings.

BACK
Using 3mm needles and A, cast on (77)81(85) sts.
Work 6cm K1, P1 rib, inc 20 sts evenly across last row. (97)101(105) sts.

Change to 4mm needles and cont in patt as set for (1st)3rd(1st) sizes of right front and keeping the sequence of colours correct, until work measures (22)23(24)cm from top of rib, ending on the same patt row as front at armhole.
Shape armholes
Cast off 4 sts at beg of next 2 rows, then 2 sts at beg of foll 4 rows. Now dec 1 st at each end of foll alt row. (79)83(87) sts.
Work straight until armhole matches front to shoulder.
Shape shoulders
Cast off 8 sts at beg of next 2 rows, then (8)9(10) sts at beg of foll 4 rows.
Cast off rem 31 sts.

SLEEVES
Using 3mm needles and A, cast on (39)41(45) sts.
Work 8cm K1, P1 rib, inc 12 sts evenly across last row. (51)53(57) sts.
Change to 4mm needles and cont in patt as given for (2nd)3rd(1st) size of front and beg with a band of B on C, *at the same time*, inc 1 st at each end of every foll 6th row until there are (81)85(89) sts.
Work straight until sleeve measures (35)36(37)cm from top of rib, ending on same patt row as front at armhole.
Shape top
Cast off 2 sts at beg of next 2 rows, then dec 1 st at each end of every foll alt row until there are (57)61(65) sts.
Now dec 1 st at each end of 5 foll 4th rows.
Cast off 2 sts at beg of foll (4)6(8) rows, then 3 sts at beg of foll 2 rows. 33 sts.
Cast off.

FRONT AND NECK BORDER
Using 3mm needles and A, cast on 7 sts.
Work (1)2(3)cm K1, P1 rib.
Make buttonhole:
Next row Rib 3, yfwd, K2 tog, rib to end.
Cont in rib making 4 more buttonholes at 6cm intervals, until band when slightly stretched fits left and right front opening edge and back neck.
Cast off in rib.

MAKING UP
Join side and shoulder seams. Join sleeve seams. Set in sleeves gathering sleeve top to fit and matching jacquard patt. Sew on front and neck border.
Sew on buttons.

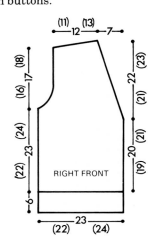

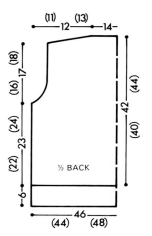

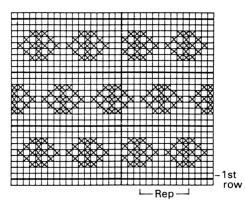

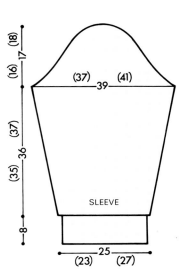

Photograph: Maury   Designed by Sophie Serret

Checkmate

Super-sophisticated cardigan with an all-over check pattern and geometric yoke. A narrow fitting garment worked in very fine yarn.

AUTUMN
★ ★

SIZES
To fit (76)81(86)cm bust

MATERIALS
(250)300(300)g three-ply yarn in main colour (A)
(200)250(250)g in contrast colour (B)
1 pair 2¼mm needles
7 buttons

TENSION
34 sts and 41 rows to 10cm over patt on 2¼mm needles.

RIGHT FRONT
Using A, cast on (67)71(75) sts.
Work 4cm K1, P1 rib, ending with a WS row.
Make buttonhole:
1st buttonhole row Rib 4, cast off 2 sts, rib to end.
2nd buttonhole row Rib to end, casting on 2 sts over those cast off in previous row.
Cont in rib until work measures 7cm from beg, ending with a WS row.
Next row Rib 10, sl these sts on to safety pin, K to end, inc 12 sts evenly across row. (69)73(77) sts.
Next row With B, P to end.
Commence patt from chart 1:
1st row (RS) K1B, *2B, 3A, 1B; rep from * to last (2)0(4) sts, (2B)0(2B, 2A)
2nd row P (1A, 1B)0(1B, 2A, 1B), *2A, 1B; rep from * to last st, 1A.
These 2 rows set the position of chart 1.
Cont working from chart 1, inc 1 st at side seam edge on every foll 12th row until there are (72)76(80) sts.
Work straight until front measures (22)23(24)cm from top of rib, ending with a RS row.
Shape armhole
Cast off 8 sts at beg of next row and 2 sts at beg of 3 foll alt rows. Now dec 1 st at beg of next alt row. (57)61(65) sts.
Work straight until front measures approx (34)37(40)cm from top of rib, ending with a 6th patt row.
Commence patt from chart 2:
1st row (RS) K1B, *1B, 1A, 4B; rep from * to last (2)0(4) sts, (1A, 1B)0(1B, 1A, 2B).
2nd row P(1B, 1A)0(1B, 1A, 1B, 1A), *3B, 1A, 1B, 1A; rep from * to last st, 1B.
These 2 rows establish the position of chart 2.
Cont working from chart 2 until front measures (37)39(41)cm, ending with a WS row.
Shape neck
Cast off 5 sts at beg of next and foll alt row, then 2 sts at beg of foll 6 alt rows.
Now dec 1 st at neck edge on next alt row. (34)38(42) sts.

Work straight until armhole measures (21)22(23)cm from beg, ending with a RS row. (Cont in B only when chart 2 is complete.)
Shape shoulder
Cast off (9)10(11) sts at beg of next and foll alt row. Cast off (8)9(10) sts at beg of next alt row.
Work 1 row.
Cast off rem (8)9(10) sts.

LEFT FRONT
Work as given for right front omitting buttonhole and reversing patts from chart 1 and 2 and all shapings.

BACK
Using A, cast on (102)110(118) sts.
Work 7cm K1, P1 rib, ending with a WS row.
Next row K to end, inc 19 sts evenly across the row. (121)129(137) sts.
Next row With B, P to end.
Commence patt from chart 1:
1st row (RS) K(0)1B(1A, 1B), *2B, 3A, 1B; rep from * to last (1)2(3) sts, (1B)2B(2B, 1A).
2nd row P(1B)1A, 1B, (2A, 1B), *2A, 1B; rep from * to last (0)1(2) sts, (0)1A(2A).
These 2 rows establish the position of chart 1. Cont in patt from chart 1, inc 1 st at each end of every foll 12th row until there are (127)135(143) sts.
Work straight until back measures (22)23(24)cm from top of rib, ending on same patt row as right front to armhole.
Shape armholes
Cast off 7 sts at beg of next 2 rows. Now dec 1 st at each end of next and foll 2 alt rows. (107)115(123) sts.
Cont in patt from chart 1 until back measures approx (34)37(40)cm from top of rib, ending with a 6th patt row.
Commence patt from chart 2:
1st row (RS) K(2B)0(1B), *3B, 1A, 2B; rep from * to last (3)1(2) sts, (3B)1B(2B).
2nd row P(1A, 2B)1B(2B), *1B, 1A, 1B, 1A, 2B; rep from * to last (2)0(1) sts, (1B, 1A)0(1B).
These 2 rows establish the position of chart 2.
Cont in patt from chart 2 until armhole measures (20)21(22)cm from beg.
Shape shoulders
Cast off (9)10(11) sts at beg of next 4 rows, then (8)9(10) sts at beg of next 4 rows.
Cast off rem 39 sts.

SLEEVES
Using A, cast on (57)63(69) sts.
Work 5cm K1, P1 rib, ending with a WS row. K one row in A, P one row in B.
Work patt from chart 1 as given for 2nd size of back.

Cont in patt from chart 2, inc 1 st at each end of every foll 8th row until there are (93)99(105) sts.
Work straight until sleeve measures (37)38(39)cm from top of rib, ending on same patt row as front to armhole.
Shape top
Cast off 5 sts at beg of next 2 rows.
Work 3 rows. Dec 1 st at each end of next and 2 foll 4th rows, then dec 1 st at each end of every alt row until there are (35)39(43) sts. Now cast off (4)5(6) sts at beg of next 4 rows.
Cast off rem 19 sts.

MAKING UP
Join shoulder seams and side seams. Join sleeve seams. Set in sleeves.
Right front border
Sl 10 sts left on safety pin at top of rib on to a needle. Rejoin A.

Chart 1

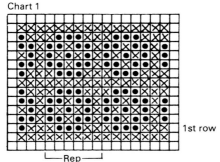

1st row

└─Rep─┘

Chart 2   ┌Rep fronts┐

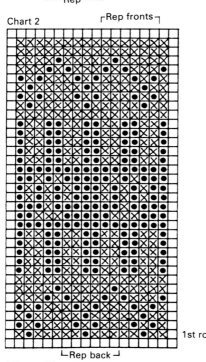

1st row

└─Rep back─┘

⊡ A   ⊠ B

Photograph: Dell'Orto   Designed by Eija

Work in K1, P1 rib, inc 1 st at inside edge on 1st row and making 5 more buttonholes as before at (6.5)7(7.5)cm intervals, until border fits up right front edge. Leave these sts on a safety pin.

Left front border

Work as given for right front border omitting buttonholes.

Neckband

With RS of work facing, using A, K across 11 sts from safety pin at right front, K up 117 sts from neck edge, K across 11 sts from safety pin at left front. 139 sts.
Work 2cm K1, P1 rib, making a buttonhole as before on 2nd row. Cast off in rib.
Join front borders to fronts.
Sew on buttons.

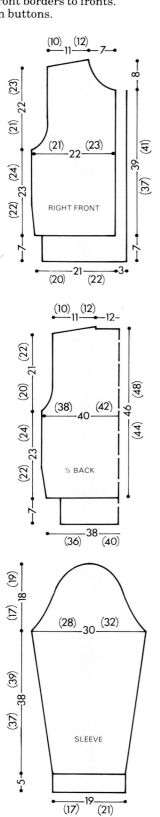

Sweatshirt

Panels of Irish moss stitch and diagonal seed stitch divide this simple sweater. Made here in a snug woollen yarn, it could also be knitted up in cotton for spring.

SIZE
To fit 86–91cm bust

MATERIALS
450g double knitting yarn
1 pair each 2¾mm, 3¼mm and 3¾mm needles

TENSION
25 sts and 28 rows to 10cm over Irish moss st on 3¾mm needles.

FRONT
Using 2¾mm needles, cast on 120 sts.
Work 7cm K2, P2, rib.
Change to 3¾mm needles and work 2 rows st st, inc 13 sts evenly across 1st row.
Commence Irish moss st and diagonal patt working from chart:
1st row (RS) Work from A to B, then C to D, then E to D, then A-F.
2nd row K all the P sts of previous row and P all the K sts.
These 2 rows set the chart patt. The chart shows RS rows only. Cont in patt working RS rows from chart, and all WS rows as given for 2nd row, until work measures 31cm from top of rib, ending with a WS row (when chart is complete, cont as set).
Shape armholes
Cast off 5 sts at beg of next 2 rows, 4 sts at beg of next 2 rows, and 3 sts at beg of foll 2 rows. 109 sts.
Now work straight until front measures 45cm from top of rib, ending with a WS row.
Divide for neck
Next row Patt 45 sts, turn, leaving rem sts on a spare needle, cont on these sts only for left side of neck.
**Cast off 7 sts at beg of next row, then 3 sts at beg of foll alt row and 2 sts at beg of foll 2 alt rows. 31 sts.
Now work 6 rows straight.
Cast off.
Return to sts on spare needle, with RS facing rejoin yarn to next st, cast off 19 sts, patt to end. Work 1 row.
Complete to match left side of neck from ** to end.

BACK
Work as given for front until back measures 6 rows less than back to shoulder, ending with a WS row.

Divide for neck
Next row Patt 45 sts, turn, leaving rem sts on a spare needle, cont on these sts only for right side of neck.
***Cast off 8 sts at beg of next row and 6 sts at beg of foll alt row. 31 sts.
Work 2 rows straight.
Cast off.
Return to sts on spare needle, with RS facing rejoin yarn to next st, cast off 19 sts, patt to end. Work 1 row.
Complete to match left side of neck working from *** to end.

SLEEVES
Using 2¾mm needles, cast on 62 sts.
Work 7cm K2, P2 rib.
Change to 3¾mm needles and work 2 rows st st, inc 9 sts evenly across 1st row. 71 sts.
Cont in patt working from chart:
1st row (RS) Work from A to D, then from A to F.
2nd row K the P sts of previous row and P the K sts.
These 2 rows set the chart patt. Cont in patt, inc 1 st at each end of every foll 8th row until there are 91 sts, then at each end of every foll 6th row until there are 99 sts.
Now work straight until sleeve measures 42cm from top of rib.
Shape top
Cast off 5 sts at beg of next 2 rows, then 4 sts at beg of foll 2 rows and 3 sts at beg of foll 2 rows. 75 sts.
Cast off.

MAKING UP
Front neck and shoulder band
Using 3¼mm needles, with RS of work facing, K up 120 sts along left shoulder, front neck and right shoulder of sweater front.
Work 4cm K2, P2 rib.
Cast off in rib.
Back neck and shoulder band ·
Using 3¼mm needles, with RS of work facing, K up 108 sts along right shoulder, back neck and left shoulder.
Work 4cm K2, P2 rib.
Cast off in rib.
Join row ends of back and front neck and shoulder bands, overlapping back band over front band.

Slipstitch the bands neatly together for about 12cm in to the neck edge allowing the overlap to taper gradually away.
Join side and sleeve seams.
Set in sleeves.

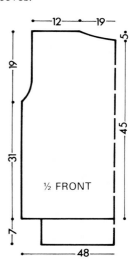

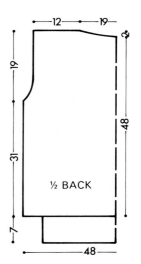

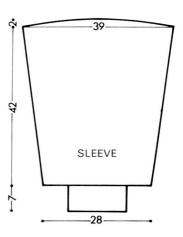

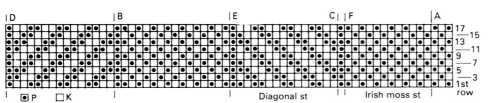

Diagonal st   Irish moss st

▣ P   □ K

Note: the chart shows RS rows only. On WS rows K all the P sts of previous row and P all the K sts.

Photograph: Sepp   Designed by Valérie Ribadeau Dumas

Cherry Ripe

An appealing bobbly cardigan with a peplum. The back is worked entirely in Irish moss stitch. The cherries are knitted in but, to make things easier, the stems and leaves are embroidered on afterwards.

WINTER
★ ★

SIZES
To fit age (4)6(8) years

MATERIALS
(250)300(350)g Aran-weight yarn in main colour (A)
50 g in each of 2 contrast colours (B, C)
1 pair each 3¾mm and 4½mm needles
6 buttons

TENSION
18 sts and 22 rows to 10cm over Irish moss st on 4½mm needles.

IRISH MOSS ST
(Over an even number of sts)
1st row (RS) *K1, P1; rep from * to end.
2nd row As 1st row.
3rd row *P1, K1; rep from * to end.
4th row As 3rd row.
These 4 rows form the patt rep.

SPECIAL ABBREVIATION
Make bobble – K into front, back, front and back again of next st, turn, P4, turn, K4, turn, P4, turn, K4, turn, sl 1, P2 tog, psso, P1, turn, K2 tog.

RIGHT FRONT
Using 4½mm needles and A, cast on (30)32(34) sts.
Work 4 rows g st. Cont in st st with moss st border:
Next row (RS) [K1, P1] twice, K to end.
Next row P to last 4 sts, [P1, K1] twice.
Rep the last 2 rows until work measures (3.5)4(4.5)cm from beg, ending with a WS row.
Make buttonhole:
Next row Moss st 1, yrn, work 2 tog, moss st 1, patt to end.
Make 4 more buttonholes at (5.5)6(6.5)cm intervals, *at the same time* cont in st st with moss st border until work measures 7cm from beg, ending with a RS row.
Change to 3¾mm needles.
Next row Work in K1, P1 rib to last 4 sts, moss st 4.
Eyelet row Moss st 4, *yon, work 2 tog, rib 3; rep from * to last (1)3(0) sts, rib to end.
Next row Patt to end, dec 4 sts evenly across the row. (26)28(30) sts.
Change to 4½mm needles and commence cherry patt:
1st row (RS) Moss st 4, K1, Irish moss st 4, K1, P11, K1, Irish moss st (4)6(8).
2nd row Irish moss st (4)6(8), P1, K11, P1, Irish moss st 4, P1, moss st 4.
3rd–4th rows Rep 1st–2nd rows once more.
5th row Moss st 4, K1, Irish moss st 4, K1, P6, make bobble in B, P4, K1, Irish moss st (4)6(8).

6th row As 2nd row.
7th row Moss st 4, K1, Irish moss st 4, K1, P4, make bobble in B, P6, K1, Irish moss st (4)6(8).
8th row As 2nd row.
Rep 1st–2nd rows (6)7(8) times.
These (20)22(24) rows form the patt rep.
Cont in patt until work measures (24)26(28)cm from beg, ending with a RS row.
Shape armhole
Cast off 2 sts at beg of next and foll alt row, then dec 1 st at armhole edge on next alt row. (21)23(25) sts.
Cont in patt until work measures (31)34(37)cm from cast-on edge, ending with a WS row.
Shape neck
Next row Moss st 4, leave these 4 sts of border on a safety pin, cast off 2 sts, patt to end.
Work 1 row.
Cast off 2 sts at beg of next and foll alt row, then dec 1 st at neck edge on next alt row. (10)12(14) sts.
Cont in patt until armhole measures (15)16(17)cm from beg.
Cast off.

LEFT FRONT
Work left front as given for right front omitting buttonholes and reversing moss st border, cherry patt and all shapings. (To reverse cherry patt, read all patt rows backwards.)

BACK
Using 4½mm needles and A, cast on (56)61(64) sts.
Work 4 rows g st. Cont in st st until work measures 7cm, ending with a RS row.
Change to 3¾mm needles and work 1 row K1, P1 rib.
Eyelet row Rib (4)1(4), *yon, work 2 tog, rib 3; rep from * to last (2)0(0) sts, rib to end of row.
Rib 1 row.
Change to 4½mm needles and cont in Irish moss st, dec (8)9(8) sts evenly across 1st row, until back measures (24)26(28)cm from beg. (48)52(56) sts.
Shape armholes
Cast off 2 sts at beg of next 4 rows, then dec 1 st at each end of foll alt row. (38)42(46) sts.
Work straight until back measures (38)41(44)cm from beg, ending with a WS row.
Divide for neck
Next row Patt (10)12(14) sts, turn, leaving rem sts on a spare needle, cont on these sts only for right side of neck.
Work straight until armhole measures (15)16(17)cm. Cast off.

Return to sts on spare needle, with RS of work facing, sl next 18 sts on to st holder, rejoin yarn to next st and complete to match right side of neck.

SLEEVES
Using 3¾mm needles and A, cast on (21)25(29) sts.
Work 3cm K1, P1 rib.
Change to 4½mm needles and commence patt:
1st row (RS) Irish moss st (4)6(8), K1, P11, K1, Irish moss st (4)6(8).
This row sets the position of the cherry patt panel.
Cont in cherry patt as for right front, but work 5th row instead of 7th row and 7th row instead of 5th row, and inc 1 st at each end of every foll (9th)10th(9th) row, working the extra sts in Irish moss st, until there are (33)37(41) sts.
Work straight until sleeve measures (28)30(32)cm from top of rib.
Shape top
Dec 1 st at each end of next and every foll alt row until (11)13(15) sts rem.
Cast off.

MAKING UP
Using C, embroider leaves and stems in stem stitch.
Join shoulder seams and side seams.
Neckband
Using 3¾mm needles and A, with RS of work facing, K 4 sts from right front st holder, K up 16 sts up right front neck, 4 sts from right back neck, K18 from back neck st holder, K up 4 sts up left back neck, 16 sts down left front neck and 4 sts from left front st holder. 66 sts.
Next row Moss st 4, P58, moss st 1, yon, work 2 tog, moss st 1.
Next row Moss st 4, K58, moss st 4.
Rep last row 3 times more. Cast off.
Join sleeve seams.
Set in sleeves.
Sew on buttons.
Make a plaited or twisted cord to thread through eyelet holes at waist and bring ends through at front to tie.

Photograph: Sepp Designed by A. Tikhomiroff

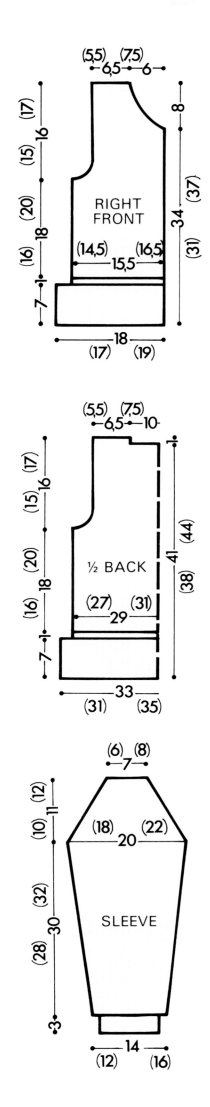

RIGHT FRONT

(5,5) (7,5)
6,5 — 6
(17) 16
(15)
(20) 18
(16)
8
34 (37)
(31)
(14,5) (16,5)
15,5
7
18
(17) (19)

½ BACK

(5,5) (7,5)
6,5 — 10
(17) 16
(15)
(20) 18
(16)
41 (44)
(38)
(27) (31)
29
7
33
(31) (35)

SLEEVE

(6) (8)
7
(12) 11
(10)
(18) (22)
20
(32) 30
(28)
3
14
(12) (16)

Baggy

A simple chunky sweater for absolute beginners. The ribbed yoke is made separately and sewn in.

SIZES
To fit (81)86(91)cm bust

MATERIALS
(950)1050(1150)g chunky yarn
1 pair each 4½mm and 5mm needles

TENSION
14 sts and 21 rows to 10cm over st st on 5mm needles.

FRONT
Using 4½mm needles, cast on (73)77(81) sts. Work 6cm K1, P2, rib.
Change to 5mm needles and cont in st st until work measures (25)26(27)cm from top of rib.
Shape armholes
Dec 1 st at each end of next and foll alt row, and at each end of 3 foll 4th rows. (63)67(71) sts.
Work straight until front measures (36)38(40)cm from top of rib, ending with a P row.
Divide for yoke
Next row Patt (31)33(35) sts, turn, leaving rem sts on a spare needle, cont on these sts only for left side of yoke.
Cast off 2 sts at beg of next row, dec 1 st at beg of foll alt row. Work 1 row.
Rep from ** to ** 7 times more.
Cast off rem (7)9(11) sts.
Return to sts on spare needle, with RS of work facing rejoin yarn to next st, cast off 1 st, patt to end.
Work 1 row.
Complete to match left side reversing shaping.

BACK
Using 4½mm needles, cast on (69)73(77) sts. Work 6cm K1, P2 rib.
Change to 5mm needles and cont in st st until the work measures (25)26(27)cm from the top of rib.

Shape armholes
Dec 1 st at each end of next and 2 foll 4th rows. (63)67(71) sts. Now work straight until back measures (46)48(50)cm from top of rib, ending with a P row.
Divide for neck
Next row Patt (31)33(35) sts, turn, leaving rem sts on a spare needle, cont on these sts only for right side of neck.
Cast off 4 sts at beg of next and foll 5 alt rows.
Cast off rem (7)9(11) sts.
Return to sts on spare needle, with RS of work facing rejoin yarn to next st, cast off 1 st, patt to end. (31)33(35) sts.
Work 1 row.
Complete to match right side, reversing shaping.

SLEEVES
Using 4½mm needles, cast on (41)44(47) sts.
Work 5cm K1, P2 rib, inc 20 sts evenly across last row. (61)64(67) sts.
Change to 5mm needles and cont in st st, inc 1 st at each end of every foll 4th row until there are (77)80(83) sts.
Work straight until sleeve measures (31)32(33)cm from top of rib.
Shape top
Cast off 5 sts at beg of next 12 rows.
Cast off rem (17)20(23) sts.

FRONT YOKE
Using 4½mm needles, cast on 67 sts.
Work in K1, P1 rib, cast off 2 sts at beg of next 32 rows.
Cast off rem 3 sts.

BACK YOKE
Using 4½mm needles, cast on 67 sts.
Work in K1, P1 rib, cast off 4 sts at beg of next 16 rows.
Cast off rem 3 sts.

MAKING UP
Set yokes into front and back, matching cast-on edge to shoulder line. Join shoulders (10)11(12)cm in from side edge. Join side and sleeve seams. Set in sleeves.

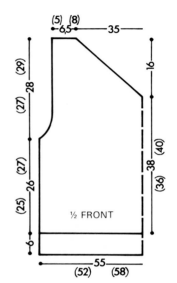

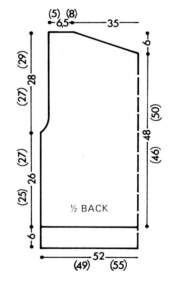

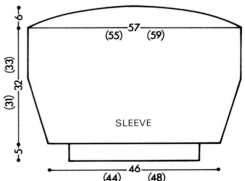

Photograph: Bouillaud   Designed by Suzuya

Winter Warmer

A real outdoor sweater in a chunky embossed stitch pattern. It has a close-fitting polo neck for added insulation.

SIZE
To fit 96–101cm chest

MATERIALS
900g Aran-weight yarn
1 pair 4mm needles
1 pair 5mm needles

TENSION
20 sts and 23 rows to 10cm over patt on 5mm needles.

FRONT
Using 4mm needles, cast on 105 sts.
Work 7cm K1, P1 rib.
Change to 5mm needles and commence embossed patt:
1st row (RS) K to end.
2nd row *K3, P1, K3, P7; rep from * to last 7 sts, K3, P1, K3.
3rd row *K3, yfwd, K1, yfwd, K3, sl 1, K1, psso, K3, K2 tog; rep from * to last 7 sts, K3, yfwd, K1, yfwd, K3.
4th row *K3, P1 tbl into yfwd of previous row, P1, P1 tbl, K3, P5; rep from * to last 9 sts, K3, P1 tbl, P1, P1 tbl, K3.
5th row *K3, [yfwd, K3] twice, sl 1, K1, psso, K1, K2 tog; rep from * to last 9 sts, K3, [yfwd, K3] twice.
6th row *K3, P1 tbl, P3, P1 tbl, K3, P3; rep from * to last 11 sts, K3, P1 tbl, P3, P1 tbl, K3.
7th row *K3, yfwd, K5, yfwd, K3, sl 2 tog K-wise, K1, p2sso; rep from * to last 11 sts, K3, yfwd, K5, yfwd, K3.
8th row *K3, P1 tbl, P5, P1 tbl, K3, P1; rep from * to last 13 sts, K3, P1 tbl, P5, P1 tbl, K3.
9th row *K3, sl 1, K1, psso, K3, K2 tog, K3, yfwd, K1, yfwd; rep from * to last 13 sts, K3, sl 1, K1, psso, K3, K2 tog, K3.
10th row *K3, P5, K3, P1 tbl, P1, P1 tbl; rep from * to last 11 sts, K3, P5, K3.
11th row *K3, sl 1, K1, psso, K1, K2 tog, [K3, yfwd] twice; rep from * to last 11 sts, K3, sl 1, K1, psso, K1, K2 tog, K3.
12th row *K3, P3, K3, P1 tbl, P3, P1 tbl; rep from * to last 9 sts, K3, P3, K3.
13th row *K3, sl 2 tog K-wise, K1, p2sso, K3, yfwd, K5, yfwd; rep from * to last 9 sts, K3, sl 2 tog, K1, p2sso, K3.
The 2nd–13th rows form the patt rep.**
Cont in patt until the work measures 56cm from the top of the rib, ending with a WS row.

Divide for neck
Note: sts are inc by 2, 4 and 6 on 3rd, 5th and 7th patt rows and dec by 2, 4 and 6 on 9th, 11th and 13th patt rows. These extra sts should be ignored when counting sts for shaping.
Next row Patt 41 sts, turn, leaving rem sts on a spare needle, cont on these sts only for left side of neck.

Dec 1 st neck edge on next 6 rows. 35 sts.
Work straight until the front measures 59cm from the top of the rib, ending with a WS row.
Shape shoulder
Cast off 7 sts at beg of next and foll 3 alt rows.
Work 1 row.
Cast off rem 7 sts.
Return to sts on spare needle, with RS of work facing rejoin yarn to next st, cast off 23 sts, patt to end. 41 sts.
Complete to match left side of neck reversing all shapings.

BACK
Work as given for the front of the sweater to **.
Cont in patt until work matches front to shoulder ending with a WS row.
Divide for neck and shape shoulders
Next row Cast off 7 sts, patt 32 including st used to cast off, work 2 tog, turn, leaving rem sts on a spare needle, cont on these sts only for right side of neck. 33 sts.
Next row Work 2 tog, patt to end. 32 sts.
Next row Cast off 7 sts, patt to last 2 sts, work 2 tog. 24 sts.
Rep last 2 rows once more, then the first one again. 14 sts.
Cast off 7 sts at beg of next row.
Work 1 row.
Cast off rem 7 sts.
Return to sts on spare needle, with RS of work facing rejoin yarn to next st, cast off 23 sts, patt to end. 41 sts.
Next row Cast off 7 sts, patt to last 2 sts, work 2 tog. 33 sts.
Next row Work 2 tog, patt to end. 32 sts.
Rep last 2 rows twice more. 14 sts.
Next row Cast off 7 sts, patt to end.
Work 1 row.
Cast off rem 7 sts.

SLEEVES
Using 4mm needles, cast on 58 sts.
Work 8cm K1, P1 rib, inc 11 sts evenly across last row. 69 sts.
Change to 5mm needles and work in patt as given for front, beg with an 8th patt row, until sleeve measures 20cm from top of rib.
Now inc 1 st at each end of next and every foll 10th row until there are 77 sts on the needle.
Work straight until sleeve measures 42cm from top of rib.
Cast off.

COLLAR
Using 4mm needles, cast on 106 sts.
Work 21cm K1, P1 rib.
Cast off loosely in rib.

MAKING UP
Join shoulder seams.
Set sleeves in flat, matching centre of cast-off edge of sleeve to shoulder seam.
Join side and sleeve seams.
Join collar seam.
Sew cast-off edge of collar to neck edge.

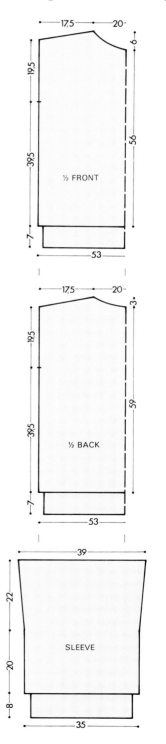

Photograph: Deconinck   Designed by Pierrette Guillot

Dotty

A sweet little fluffy sweater that makes a really cosy cover-up. Make it in a plain yarn for children with sensitive skin.

SIZES
To fit age (4)6(8) years

MATERIALS
(200)250(250)g Aran-weight yarn in main colour (A)
50g in contrast colour (B)
1 pair each 4mm and 4½mm needles
1 set four double-pointed 4mm needles

TENSION
19 sts and 21 rows to 10cm over patt on 4½mm needles.

FRONT
Using 4mm needles and A, cast on (47)51(55) sts.
Work 4cm K1, P1 rib, inc 8 sts evenly across last row. (55)59(63) sts.
Change to 4½mm needles and commence patt:
1st row (RS) K to end.
2nd row P to end.
3rd row *K3A, 1B; rep from * to last 3 sts, K3A.
4th row P to end.
5th row K to end.
6th row P1A, *1B, 3A; rep from * to last 2 sts, 1B, 1A.·
These 6 rows form the patt rep.**
Cont in patt until front measures (19)21(23)cm from top of rib, ending with a WS row.
Divide for neck
Next row Patt (27)29(31) sts, turn, leaving rem sts on a spare needle, cont on these sts only for left side of neck.
Dec 1 st at beg of next and foll 2 alt rows. (24)26(28) sts.
Shape armhole
Cast off 4 sts at beg of next row.
Now keeping armhole edge straight, dec 1 st at neck edge on every alt row until (14)16(18) sts rem.
Work straight until armhole measures (12)13(14)cm from beg of armhole

shaping, ending at armhole edge. Cast off.
Return to sts on spare needle, with RS of work facing rejoin yarn to centre st, cast off 1 st, patt to end.
Patt 1 row.
Complete to match left side of neck.

BACK
Work as given for front to **.
Cont in patt until back matches front to armhole.
Shape armholes
Cast off 4 sts at beg of next 2 rows. (47)51(55) sts.
Now work straight until armhole measures (12)13(14)cm from beg.
Cast off.

SLEEVES
Using 4mm needles and A, cast on (24)28(32) sts.
Work 4cm K1, P1 rib, inc 3 sts evenly across last row. (27)31(35) sts.
Change to 4½mm needles.
Work in patt as given for front, inc 1 st at each end of every 5th row until there are (45)49(53) sts.
Now work straight until sleeve measures (28)30(32)cm from top of rib.
Cast off.

MAKING UP
Join shoulder seams. Set sleeves in flat matching centre of cast-off edge to shoulder seam and joining top 2cm on each side of sleeve to cast-off sts at underarm.
Neckband
Using double-pointed 4mm needles and A, beg at centre front neck, K up (80)84(88) sts around neck edge. Work in rows.
Work 4 rows K1, P1 rib.
Cast off in rib.
Join row ends of neckband to front, overlapping right edge over left.
Join side seams.

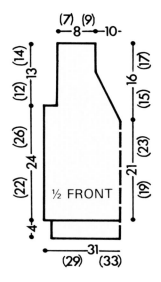

½ FRONT

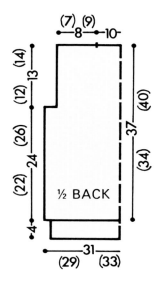

½ BACK

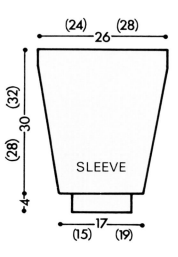

SLEEVE

Photograph: Bensimon   Designed by Sophie Serret

Crazy Colour

Zigzag and diamond patterns in a clutch of brilliant primary colours on a thick-knit raglan cardigan.

SIZES
To fit (81)86(91)cm bust

MATERIALS
(400)450(500)g Aran-weight yarn in main colour (A)
(200)200(250)g in 1st contrast colour (B)
100g in 2nd contrast colour (C)
50g in each of 3rd and 4th contrast colours (D, E)
1 pair each 4mm and 5mm needles
7 buttons

TENSION
19 sts and 22 rows to 10cm over patt on 5mm needles.

RIGHT FRONT
Using 4mm needles and A, cast on (51)53(55) sts. Work (8)6(4) rows K1, P1 rib.
Make buttonhole:
Next row (RS) Rib 3, cast off 2 sts, rib to end of row.
Next row Rib to end, casting on 2 sts over those cast off in previous row.
Cont in rib until work measures 4cm from beg, ending with a WS row. Change to 5mm needles and work 2 rows st st.
Commence colour patt from chart 1:
1st row (RS) With A, [K1, P1] 4 times, K2A, *2A, 1C, 7A; rep from * to last (1)3(5) sts, (1A)2A, 1C(2A, 1C, 2A).
2nd row P(1A)2C, 1A(1A, 3C, 1A), *6A, 3C, 1A; rep from * to last 10 sts, 2A, with A, [K1, P1] 4 times.

These 2 rows set the position of the chart patt and rib border.
Cont in patt working from chart 1, keeping border correct make buttonholes as before at (8)8.5(9)cm intervals. When all 38 rows of chart 1 have been worked,

rep 21st–38th rows once more, then 21st–29th rows again. Now work 28th row again. Keeping rib border correct, commence colour patt from chart 2:
1st row Rib 8A, K3A, *1D, 9A; rep from * to last (0)2(4) sts, (0)1D, 1A(1D, 3A).

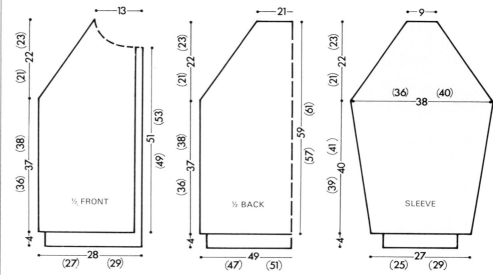

□ A   ⊡ D
⊠ B   ■ E
⊡ C

Chart 1

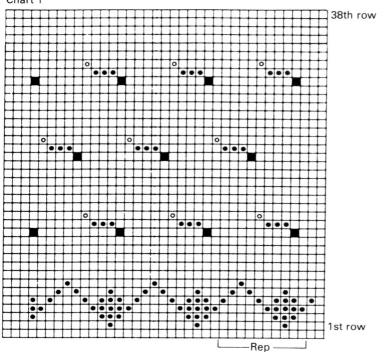

38th row

1st row

⌐ Rep ¬

Chart 2

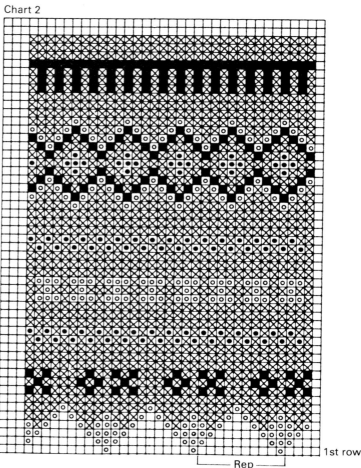

1st row

⌐ Rep ¬

Photograph: J.-B. Maudin   Designed by Catherine de Chabaneix

2nd row (0)2D(2A, 2D), *1D, 7A, 2D; rep
from * to last 11 sts, 1D, 2A, rib 8A.
These 2 rows set the position of the patt.
Cont in patt from chart 2 until work
measures (36)37(38)cm from top of rib,
ending with a RS row.

Shape raglan armhole and neck
Keeping chart patt correct, cast off 2 sts at
beg of next and foll (2)3(4) alt rows, then
dec 1 st at armhole edge on foll 20 alt
rows, *at the same time*, when work
measures (49)51(53)cm from top of rib, sl
17 sts at neck edge on to a st holder, then
cast off 2 sts at neck edge on next and foll
3 alt rows (when colour patt from chart 2
is complete, cont in st st in B only).
Fasten off.

LEFT FRONT
Work as given for right front reversing
ribbed border, patt from charts, and all
shapings, and omitting buttonholes.

BACK
Using 4mm needles and A, cast on
(87)93(97) sts.
Work 4cm K1, P1 rib. Change to 5mm
needles and work 2 rows st st.
Now work colour patt from charts 1 and 2
as given for (3rd)1st(3rd) size of right
front, omitting the 8 rib sts in A, until
work measures (36)37(38)cm from top of
rib, ending on same patt row as right front
to armhole.

Shape raglan armholes
Cast off (1)2(2) sts at beg of next (2)4(6)
rows, then dec 1 st at each end of next and
every foll alt row until 41 sts rem.
Cast off.

SLEEVES
Using 4mm needles and A, cast on
(47)53(55) sts.
Work 4cm K1, P1 rib. Change to 5mm
needles and work 2 rows st st.
Cont in patt from chart 1 as set for
(3rd)1st(2nd) size of right front, omitting
the 8 rib sts in A, inc 1 st at each end of
(11)10(11) foll 6th rows. (69)73(77) sts.
When all 38 rows of chart 1 have been
worked rep 21st–38th rows twice more.
Now cont in patt from chart 2 until sleeve
measures approx (39)40(41)cm from top of
rib, ending on same patt row as right front
to armhole.

Shape top
Cast off 2 sts at beg of foll (6)8(10) rows,
then dec 1 st at each end of next and every
foll alt row until 17 sts rem (when colour
patt from chart 2 is complete cont in st st
in B only).
Cast off.

MAKING UP
Join raglan seams.

Neckband
Using 4mm needles and A, with RS of
work facing, beg at right front neck edge,
K across 17 sts from st holder, K up 8 sts
from neck edge, K up 77 sts across top of
sleeve, back neck edge and top of left
sleeve, K up 8 sts down left neck edge, K
across 17 sts on st holder. 127 sts.
Work 1 row K1, P1 rib.
Rib 2 rows making buttonhole as given for
right front. Cont in rib until neckband
measures 3cm from beg.
Cast off in rib.
Join side and sleeve seams.
Sew on buttons.

Sporty

A polo-necked sweater, just right for the outdoor life, is worked in an Aran yarn and livened with a band of simple jacquard.

SIZES
To fit (81)86(91)cm bust

MATERIALS
(600)650(650)g Aran-weight yarn in main colour (A)
200g in 1st contrast colour (B)
50g in each of 2nd and 3rd contrast colours (C, D)
1 pair 4mm needles
1 pair 5mm needles
1 set four double-pointed 4mm needles

TENSION
18 sts and 22 rows to 10cm over st st on 5mm needles.

FRONT
Using 4mm needles and A, cast on (91)95(99) sts.
Work 9cm K1, P1 rib.
Change to 5mm needles and work in st st, inc 6 sts evenly across 1st row.
(97)101(105) sts.
Cont in st st until front measures (35)36(37)cm from top of rib, ending with a WS row.
Commence jacquard patt from chart:
1st row (RS) K1A, [1A, 3C, 3A, 1C, 2A] (9)10(10) times, (1A, 3C, 2A)0(1A, 3C).
2nd row P(3A, 1C, 2A)0(1A, 1C, 2A), [2A, 1D, 4A, 1C, 2A] (9)10(10) times, 1A.
These 2 rows set the position of the patt.
Cont in patt working from chart.**
When all 12 rows of chart have been worked cont in st st in B until front measures (48)50(52)cm from top of rib, ending with a WS row.
Divide for neck
Next row K(42)44(46), turn, leaving rem sts on a spare needle, cont on these sts only for left side of neck.
***Cast off 4 sts at beg of next row, 3 sts at beg of foll alt row and 2 sts at beg of next alt row. (33)35(37) sts.
Now dec 1 st at neck edge on foll 3 alt rows. (30)32(34) sts.
Work 4 rows straight.
Cast off.
Return to sts on spare needle, with RS of work facing rejoin yarn to next st.
Next row Cast off 13 sts, K to end.
(42)44(46) sts.
Work 1 row.
Complete to match left side of neck working from *** to end.

BACK
Work as given for front to **.
When all 12 rows of chart have been worked cont in st st in B until back measures (53)55(57)cm from top of rib, ending with a WS row.
Cast off evenly.

SLEEVES
Using 4mm needles and A, cast on (39)43(47) sts.
Work 12cm K1, P1 rib.
Change to 5mm needles and work in st st, inc 6 sts evenly across first row.
(45)49(53) sts.
Cont in st st inc 1 st at each end of every foll 6th row until there are (61)65(69) sts, ending with a WS row.
Commence jacquard patt:
1st size
Work as for 2nd size front, rep patt 6 times instead of 10.
2nd size
Work as for 3rd size front, rep patt 6 times instead of 10.
3rd size
1st row (RS) K1A, [1A, 3C, 3A, 1C, 2A] 6 times, 1A, 3C, 3A, 1C.
2nd row P1D, 4A, 1C, 2A, [2A, 1D, 4A, 1C, 2A] 6 times, 1A.
These 2 rows set the position of the patt.
All sizes
Cont in patt working from chart, inc 1 st at each end of 6th and 12th chart rows.
When all 12 rows of chart have been worked, cont in st st in B, inc 1 st at each end of every foll 6th row until there are (69)73(77) sts.
Now work straight until sleeve measures (39)40(41)cm from top of rib, ending with a WS row.
Cast off.

MAKING UP
Join shoulder seams. Set sleeves in flat, matching centre of cast-off edge to shoulder seam.
Collar
Using double-pointed 4mm needles and A, with RS of work facing, K up 96 sts around neck edge.
Work in rounds.
Work 6cm K1, P1 rib.
Next row (Rib 4, work 3 times·into next st, rib 3) 12 times. 120 sts.
Cont in rib until collar measures 21cm.
Cast off in rib.
Join side and sleeve seams.

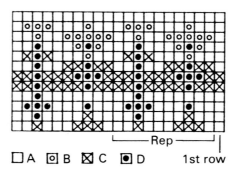

□ A ⊡ B ⊠ C ⊙ D   1st row

Rep

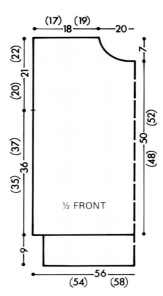

(17) (19)
18 — 20 —
(22)
21 (20) 7
(35) 36 (37)
50 (52)
(48)
½ FRONT
9
56
(54) (58)

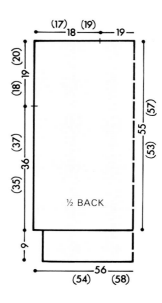

(17) (19)
18 — 19 —
(20)
19 (18)
(37)
(35) 36
55 (57)
(53)
½ BACK
9
56
(54) (58)

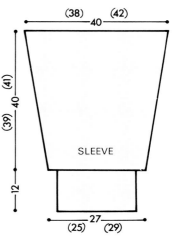

(38) (42)
40
(41)
40
(39)
SLEEVE
12
27
(25) (29)

Photograph: J.-C. Benoit   Designed by Alain Piédelièvre

Norwegian Classic

A traditional sweater worked in the round with authentic Scandinavian star and reindeer motifs. It's certainly complicated but the thick yarn means it should knit up fairly quickly.

WINTER

★ ★ ★

SIZE
To fit 96–101cm chest
Actual width 114cm
Length 68cm
Sleeve seam 55cm

MATERIALS
900g Aran-weight yarn in main colour (A)
100g in 1st contrast colour (B)
50g in 2nd contrast colour (C)
1 each circular 3mm and 4½mm needle
1 set each four double-pointed 3mm and 4½mm needles
1 pair each 3mm and 4½mm needles

TENSION
19 sts and 26 rows to 10cm over st st on 4½mm needles.

BACK AND FRONT (one piece)
Using 3mm circular needle and A, cast on 204 sts.
Work in rounds.
Work 8cm K1, P1 rib.
Change to 4½mm circular needle.
Commence dot patt:
1st–5th rounds K to end in A.
6th round *K5A, 1B; rep from * to end.
7th–11th rounds K to end in A.
12th round *K2A, 1B, 3A; rep from * to end of row.
These 12 rounds form the patt rep.
Cont in dot patt for 4 rounds.
Next round [K up loop between last st and next st to make 1, K1, make 1, K101] twice. 208 sts.
Cont in dot patt inc 1 st each side of same st as before on 2 foll 8th rows. 216 sts.
Cont in dot patt until work measures approx 29cm from top of rib, ending with a 5th or 11th patt round.
Commence patt from chart:
1st round *K1C, 5A; rep from * to end.
2nd round *K1A, 1C, 3A, 1C; rep from * to end.
These 2 rounds establish the chart patt.
Cont in patt from chart, work 2nd–10th rounds.
11th round *K1A, [1B, 4A, 1B, 1A, 1B, 1A, 1B, 7A] 3 times, 1B, 1A, 1B, [7A, 1B, 1A, 1B, 1A, 1B, 4A, 1B] 3 times, 2A; rep from * once more.
12th round *K1A, [1B, 4A, 1B, 1A, 1B, 1A, 1B, 3A, 1B, 3A] twice, 1B, 4A, [1B, 1A] twice, 1B, 8A, 1B, 8A, [1B, 1A, 1B, 1A, 1B, 4A, 1B, 3A, 1B, 3A] twice, [1B, 1A] twice, 1B, 4A, 1B, 2A; rep from * once more.
These 2 rounds establish the position of the reindeer motifs on front and back.
Cont in patt working from chart, work 13th–14th rounds.
Divide for armholes
Change to pair 4½mm needles.

Next row Patt 108 sts, turn, leaving rem sts on a spare needle, cont on these sts only for front.
Work 16th–38th rows from chart.
39th row K6B, [2B, 1A, 2B, 1A, 5B, 3A, 3B, 3A, 5B, 1A, 2B, 1A, 3B] 3 times, 6B.
40th row P6B, [2B, 2A, 1B, 3A, 3B, 2A, 2B, 1A, 1B, 1A, 2B, 2A, 3B, 3A, 1B, 2A, 1B] 3 times, 6B.
These 2 rows establish position of star motifs, cont working from chart, work 41st–76th rows. Now work 4 rows st st in C.
Shape shoulders
Cast off 42 sts at beg of next 2 rows. 24 sts.
Neckband
Work 1cm st st. Cast off.
Return to sts on spare needle, rejoin yarn to RH edge and work back to match front.

SLEEVES
Using 3mm double-pointed needles and A, cast on 54 sts. Work 8cm K1, P1 rib in rounds. Change to 4½mm needles. Work 11 rounds dot patt as for front and back.

Next round Make 1, K1, make 1, patt to end. 56 sts.
Cont in dot patt, inc 1 st each side of same st on every foll 5th round until there are 92 sts, *at the same time*, when work measures approx 29cm from top of rib, ending with a 5th or 11th patt round, work 30th–76th rounds from chart.
Work 4 rows st st in A. Cast off.

SHOULDER GUSSETS (make 2)
Using pair 3mm needles and C, cast on 23 sts. Work K1, P1 rib, dec 1 st at each end of every 4th row until there are 7 sts, now dec 1 st each end of 2 foll alt rows. 3 sts.
Next row K3 tog. Fasten off.

MAKING UP
Join shoulder seams working a backstitch seam on RS to 12cm in from armhole edge. Set in sleeves, working a backstitch seam on RS. Set shoulder gussets into neck opening on each side. Fold over neckbands to inside and catch down.

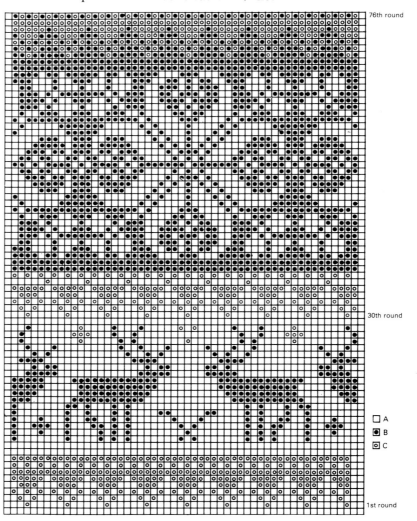

76th round

30th round

1st round

□ A
◙ B
◪ C

Photograph: C. Duffy Designed by Simone Vassort

Batwing

**A wonderfully extravagant
sweater very cleverly shaped to
produce huge batwing sleeves.
Worked in reverse stocking stitch
in flaming angora**

WINTER

★ ★

SIZES
To fit (81)86(91)cm bust

MATERIALS
(360)380(400)g medium-weight angora
1 pair each 3¾mm, 4½mm and 5½mm
needles

TENSION
16 sts and 23 rows to 10cm over reverse st
st on 5½mm needles.

FRONT
Using 3¾mm needles, cast on (86)90(94)
sts. Work 7cm K2, P2 rib.
Cast off 10 sts at beg of next 2 rows.
Change to 5½mm needles. Cont in reverse
st st, dec 10 sts evenly over 1st row, until
work measures (49.5)51.5(53.5)cm from
top of rib. (56)60(64) sts.
Change to 4½mm needles and work 2.5cm
K2, P2 rib. Cast off loosely in rib.

BACK
Work as given for front.

RIGHT SIDE AND SLEEVE
Join back and front at shoulders on each
side of cast-off edges to a point 1cm in
from side edges.
Using 4½mm needles, with RS of work
facing, K up (93)97(101) sts between top of
lower rib on back and shoulder seam, then
K up (93)97(101) sts between shoulder
seam on front and top of lower rib.
(186)194(202) sts. Work 2cm K2, P2 rib.
 Change to 5½mm needles. Cont in reverse
 st st, dec 16 sts evenly across 1st row.
(170)178(186) sts. Work straight until
side measures 4cm from top of rib.
Shape sleeve
Cast off (20)22(24) sts at beg of next 2
rows, then 2 sts at beg of foll 6 rows.
(118)122(126) sts. Now dec 1 st each end
next and every foll alt row until (78)82(86)
sts rem. Dec 1 st each end 3 foll 4th rows,
and 1 st each end every foll alt row until
(52)56(60) sts rem, then 1 st each end of 3
foll 4th rows. (46)50(54) sts.
Now work straight until work measures
(50)51(52)cm from K up row.
Change to 3¾mm needles and work 7cm
K2, P2 rib, dec 6 sts evenly over 1st row.
Cast off rem (40)44(48) sts in rib.

LEFT SIDE AND SLEEVE
Work as for right side and sleeve but K up
sts beg at top of lower rib on front and
ending at top of lower rib on back.

MAKING UP
Join cast-off edges of lower rib on back
and front to lower part of side and sleeve
pieces. Join side and sleeve seams.

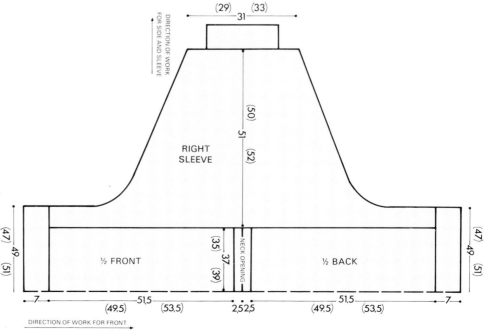

Photograph: Sepp   Designed by Brigitte Charoy

Lumberjack

A sturdy sweater made in a crunchy flecked yarn for boys or girls. Easy and quick to make.

WINTER

★

SIZES
To fit age (4)6(8) years

MATERIALS
(300)350(400)g double knitting yarn
1 pair 4mm needles

TENSION
24 sts and 28 rows to 10cm over patt on 4mm needles.

FRONT
Cast on (64)70(76) sts.
Work 5cm K1, P1 rib, inc 9 sts evenly across last row. (73)79(85) sts.
Commence patt:
1st row (RS) P1, *K2, P1; rep from * to end of row.
2nd row K1, *P2, K1; rep from * to end.
3rd row As 1st row.
4th row K to end.
These 4 rows form the patt rep.**
Cont in patt until work measures (3)4(5)cm from top of rib, ending with a WS row.
Place pocket openings
Next row Patt (16)19(22) sts, turn, leaving rem sts on a spare needle, cont on these sts only for LH side of pocket.
Cont in patt for 9cm ending with a RS row, leave these sts on a st holder.
Return to sts on spare needle, with RS of work facing rejoin yarn to next st.
Next row Patt 41 sts, turn, leaving rem sts on a st holder, cont on these sts only for pocket front.
Cont in patt for 9cm, ending with a RS row, leave these sts on a spare needle.
Return to sts on second st holder, with RS of work facing, rejoin yarn to next st and work in patt for 9cm, ending with a RS row.
Next row Patt (16)19(22) sts, now patt across 41 sts left on spare needle, now patt across (16)19(22) sts left on first st holder. (73)79(85) sts.
Now work straight until front measures (21)23(25)cm from top of rib, ending with a WS row.
Shape armholes
Cast off 5 sts at beg of next 2 rows. (63)69(75) sts.
Divide for neck
Next row Patt (26)29(32) sts, turn, leaving rem sts on a spare needle, cont on these sts only for left side of neck.
***Work straight until front measures (31)34(37)cm from top of rib, ending at neck edge.
Shape neck
Cast off 3 sts at beg of next row and 2 sts at beg of foll alt row.
Work 1 row. Now dec 1 st at beg of next and foll 2 alt rows. (18)21(24) sts.

Work straight until armhole measures (14)15(16)cm from beg.
Cast off.
Return to sts on spare needle, with RS of work facing, rejoin yarn to next st.
Next row Cast off 11 sts, patt to end. (26)29(32) sts.
Complete to match left side of neck working from *** to end.

BACK
Work as given for front to **.
Cont in patt until work measures (21)23(25)cm from top of rib, ending with a WS row.
Shape armholes
Cast off 5 sts at beg of next 2 rows. (63)69(75) sts.
Work straight until armhole measures (14)15(16)cm from beg.
Cast off.

SLEEVES
Cast on (31)37(43) sts.
Work 5cm K1, P1 rib, inc 9 sts evenly across last row. (40)46(52) sts.
Cont in patt as given for front, inc 1 st at each end of every 4th row until there are (64)68(72) sts.
Now work straight until sleeve measures (26)28(30)cm from top of rib.
Shape top
Cast off 5 sts at beg of next 8 rows. (24)28(32) sts.
Cast off.

POCKET LINING
Cast on 16 sts. Work 16cm st st.
Cast off.

NECK BORDER AND COLLAR
Cast on 11 sts.
Work (10)11(12)cm K1, P1 rib, leave these sts on a st holder.
Cast on 11 sts and work (10)11(12)cm K1, P1 rib as before.
Work collar
Next row Patt to end, turn, cast on 57 sts, turn, patt across 11 sts from st holder. 79 sts.
Work a further 6cm in rib.
Cast off loosely in rib.

MAKING UP
Join shoulder seam. Join on collar and neck borders overlapping the right border over the left one at centre front.
Pocket edgings
With RS of work facing K up 19 sts along inner edge of pocket opening. Work 2cm K1, P1 rib. Cast off in rib.
Sew down row ends of pocket edges to RS.
Sew pocket lining to WS, placing cast-on edge to outer edge of pocket opening on

RH side and cast-off edge to outer edge of pocket opening on LH side.
Join side and sleeve seams. Set in sleeves.

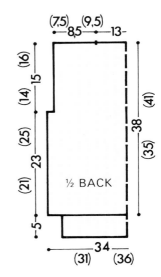

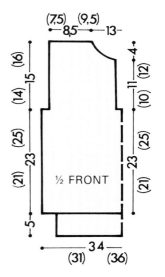

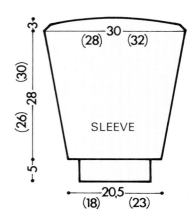

Greatcoat

Very quick to knit, using chunky yarn on thick needles and a simple fancy rib stitch pattern.

SIZES
To fit (101)106(111)cm chest

MATERIALS
(1250)1300(1350)g chunky yarn
1 pair 8mm needles
7 buttons

TENSION
10 sts and 16 rows to 10cm over patt on 8mm needles.

POCKET LININGS (make 2)
Cast on 16 sts.
Work 12cm st st, ending with a WS row, dec 1 st at each end of last row. 14 sts.
Leave these sts on a st holder.

RIGHT FRONT
Cast on (40)41(42) sts.
Commence patt:
1st row (RS) [K2, P2] to last (0)1(2) sts, K(0)1(2).
2nd row P to end.
These 2 rows form patt rep.
Cont in patt until work measures 14cm from beg, ending with a WS row.
Place pocket
Next row Patt 14 sts, leave next 14 sts on a st holder, patt 14 sts from pocket lining st holder, patt to end.**
Cont in patt until work measures (48)49(50)cm from beg, ending with a RS row.
Shape armhole
Cast off 4 sts at beg of next row and 2 sts at beg of foll alt row. Dec 1 st at armhole edge on foll 2 alt rows. (32)33(34) sts.
Now work straight until right front measures (64)66(68)cm from beg, ending with a WS row.
Shape neck
Cast off 12 sts at beg of next row, 3 sts at beg of next alt row and 2 sts at beg of foll alt row. Now dec 1 st at neck edge on foll 2 alt rows. (13)14(15) sts.
Cast off.

LEFT FRONT
Cast on (40)41(42) sts.
Commence patt:
1st row (RS) K(0)1(2), [P2, K2] to end.
2nd row P to end.
These 2 rows form patt. Cont in patt until work measures (6)5(4)cm from beg, ending with a WS row.
1st buttonhole row Patt to last 4 sts, cast off 2 sts, patt to end.
2nd buttonhole row P2, cast on 2 sts, P to end.
Cont in patt rep 2 buttonhole rows at (9.5)10(10.5)cm intervals, *at the same time* place pocket when work measures 14cm from beg, ending with a WS row.

Place pocket
Next row Patt (12)13(14) sts, leave next 14 sts on a st holder, patt 14 sts from pocket lining st holder, patt to end.
Complete to match right front reversing all shapings.

BACK
Cast on (60)62(64) sts.
Commence patt:
1st row (RS) K(1)0(1), P2, [K2, P2] to last (1)0(1) sts, K(1)0(1).
2nd row P to end.
These 2 rows from the patt rep.
Cont in patt until work measures (48)49(50)cm from beg.
Shape armholes
Cast off 4 sts at beg of next 2 rows. Dec 1 st each end of foll alt row. (50)52(54) sts.
Work straight until back measures 2 rows less than fronts to cast-off row, ending with a WS row.
Divide for neck
Next row Patt (13)14(15) sts, turn, leave rem sts on a spare needle and cont on these sts only for first side of neck.
Work 1 row. Cast off.
Return to sts on spare needle, with RS of work facing rejoin yarn to next st.
Next row Cast off 24 sts, patt to end. (13)14(15) sts.
Work 2 rows. Cast off.

SLEEVES
Cast on (32)34(36) sts. Work in patt as given for back, inc 1 st at each end of every foll 10th row until there are (46)48(50) sts.
Work straight until sleeve measures (50)51(52)cm from beg.
Shape top
Cast off 3 sts at beg of next 2 rows.
Next row Work 2 tog, patt to last 2 sts, work 2 tog.
Work 1 row.
Cast off 2 sts at beg of next 2 rows. Rep last 4 rows 3 times more. (16)18(20) sts.
Dec 1 st at each end of next alt row, then cast off (1)2(3) sts at beg of foll alt row.
Cast off rem 12 sts.

COLLAR
Cast on (65)67(69) sts.
Work 30cm K1, P1 rib.
Cast off in rib.

MAKING UP
Join shoulder seams and side seams.
Join sleeve seams and set in sleeves.
Pocket edgings
K 14 sts from st holder at pocket top.
Work 3cm K1, P1 rib. Cast off in rib.
Sew sides of pocket edgings to jacket fronts. Stitch down pocket linings.

Fold collar in half widthways. Oversew sides together neatly.
Sew collar to neck edge.
Sew on buttons.

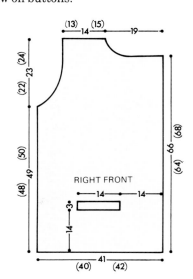

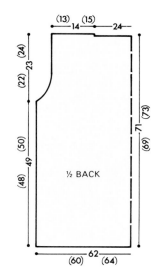

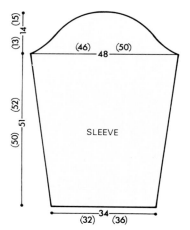

Photograph: G. Pascal   Designed by Pierre Sénac

Icelandic Sweater

**A traditional style worked entirely
in the round and including the
hallmark of Icelandic knitwear —
a circular patterned yoke.**

SIZES
To fit 86–91cm bust
Length 50cm
Sleeve seam 47cm

MATERIALS
500g chunky yarn in main colour (A)
200g in 1st contrast colour (B)
100g in 2nd contrast colour (C)
1 each 6mm and 7mm circular needle
1 set four each 6mm and 7mm
double-pointed needles

TENSION
12 sts and 16 rows to 10cm over st st on
7mm needles.

BACK AND FRONT (one piece)
Using 6mm circular needle and B, cast on
110 sts. Work in rounds.
Work 4cm K1, P1 rib.
Change to 7mm circular needle.
Next round K to end, inc 10 sts evenly
across round. 120 sts.
Commence patt from chart 1:
1st round K to end in B.
2nd round *K1A, 5B; rep from * to end.
These 2 rounds establish patt from chart
1. Work 5 more rounds from chart 1, then
cont in st st in A only until work measures
35cm from top of rib.
Next round K to last 5 sts, cut off yarn, sl
next 5 sts on to st holder.

Next round Sl next 5 sts on to same st
holder as sts from last round, sl next 50
sts on to length of yarn for back, sl next
10 sts on to st holder, sl next 50 sts on to
length of yarn for front.
Leave these sts.

SLEEVES
Using double-pointed 6mm needles and B,
cast on 32 sts.
Work in rounds.
Work 4cm K1, P1 rib.
Change to double-pointed 7mm needles.
Next round K to end, inc 4 sts evenly
across round. 36 sts.
Work 7 rounds in patt from chart 1 as
given for back and front.
Cont in st st and A only for 2 rounds.
Next round K1, K up loop between last st
and next st to make 1, K2 (mark these 2
sts), make 1, K to end of round. 38 sts.
Work 9 rounds. Inc 1 st as set each side of
2 marked sts on next and 3 foll 10th
rounds. 46 sts. Work straight until sleeve
measures 43cm from top of rib. Sl first 2
sts of next round on to RH needle, sl next
10 sts on to a st holder, sl rem 36 sts
(including first 2 sts) on to a length of yarn
for top of sleeve.
Leave these sts.

YOKE
Sl 36 sts for top of left sleeve, then 50 sts
for front, then 36 sts for top of right sleeve

and finally 50 sts for back all on to 7mm
circular needle. 172 sts.
Join on A and work 1 round, working tog
last st of each piece with first st of next
piece. 168 sts.
Commence patt from chart 2:
1st round *K3A, 1B, 2A; rep from * to
end of row.
2nd round *K1B, 2A; rep from * to end.
These 2 rounds establish patt from chart
2. Work 3rd–14th rounds.
15th round *K1A, 1B, K2 tog B, 2B; rep
from * to end. 140 sts.
Work 16th–20th rounds from chart 2 (the
black squares represent sts lost by decs
and should be ignored).
21st round *K1C, 1B, K2 tog B, 1B; rep
from * to end. 112 sts.
Work 22nd–26th rounds from chart 2.
27th round K2A, *1B, K2 tog A, 1A; rep
from * to last 2 sts, K2 tog B. 84 sts.
Work 28th–29th rounds from chart 2.
30th round *K2 tog A, 1B; rep from * to
end. 56 sts.
31st round [K1A, 1B] to end.
Change to 6mm double-pointed needles
and work 10cm K1, P1 rib.
Cast off in rib.

MAKING UP
Graft together sts left on st holders at
underarm.
Fold neck rib in half to WS of work and
slipstitch to neck edge.

Chart 1

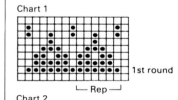

1st round
└ Rep ┘

Chart 2

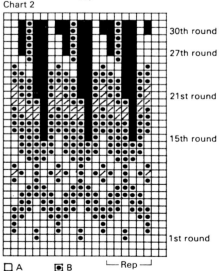

30th round
27th round
21st round
15th round
1st round
└ Rep ┘

□ A   ▣ B
◪ C   ■ Decs

Photograph: J-P. Metayer   Designed by Tricots Vanel

Snowflake

An unusual embossed cluster pattern worked in two colours is the feature of this boxy jacket.

SIZE
To fit 81–86cm bust

MATERIALS
400g four-ply yarn in main colour (A)
100g in contrast colour (B)
1 pair each 3mm and 4mm needles
12 buttons

TENSION
27 sts and 34 rows to 10cm over patt on 4mm needles.

RIGHT FRONT
Using 3mm needles and A, cast on 64 sts.
Work 5cm K1, P1 rib, inc 4 sts evenly across last row. 68 sts.
Change to 4mm needles and commence patt:
1st row (RS) K to end.
2nd, 4th and 6th rows P to end.
3rd row K1, sl 1, K1, psso, *K6, sl 1, K1, psso; rep from * to last st, K1.
5th row K2, *sl 1, K1, psso, K2, K2 tog, K1; rep from * to last st, K1.
7th row With B, sl 1 P-wise, [K1, P1, K1] into next st, *ybk, sl 4 P-wise, [K1, P1] twice into next st; rep from * to last 6 sts, ybk, sl 4 P-wise, [K1, P1, K1] into next st, K1.
8th row With B, sl all the A sts P-wise, and K all the B sts, stranding yarn on WS of work.
9th row K to end in A.
10th, 12th and 14th rows P to end in A.
11th row With A, K5, *sl 1, K1, psso, K6; rep from * to last 7 sts, sl 1, K1, psso, K5.
13th row K3, *K2 tog, K1, sl 1, K1, psso, K2; rep from * to last st, K1.
15th row With B, *ybk, sl 4 P-wise, [K1, P1] twice into next st; rep from * to last 4 sts, ybk, sl 4 P-wise.
16th row As 8th row.
These 16 rows form the patt rep.
Cont in patt until work measures 28cm from top of rib, ending with a RS row.
Shape armhole
(*Note:* when counting rows between decs, count rows in A only.)
Cast off 5 sts at beg of next row, 4 sts at beg of foll alt row and 3 sts at beg of foll alt row, then dec 1 st at beg of 4 foll alt rows. 52 sts (do not count incs and decs which occur as part of patt when making st checks throughout).
Work straight until front measures 42cm from top of rib, ending with a WS row.
Shape neck
Cast off 10 sts at beg of next row, then 2 sts at beg of 3 foll alt rows. Now dec 1 st at neck edge on foll 3 rows.
Work straight until armhole measures 19cm from beg, ending at armhole edge.

Shape shoulder
Cast off 11 sts at beg of next and foll alt row. Work 1 row.
Cast off rem 11 sts.

LEFT FRONT
Work as given for right front reversing all shapings.

BACK
Using 3mm needles and A, cast on 116 sts.
Work 5cm K1, P1 rib.
Change to 4mm needles and cont in patt as given for right front until work measures 28cm from top of rib.
Shape armholes
Cast off 3 sts at beg of next 2 rows, then 2 sts at beg of foll 6 rows.
Now dec 1 st at each end of foll 3 alt rows. 92 sts.
Work straight until armhole measures 19cm from beg.
Shape shoulders
Cast off 11 sts at beg of next 6 rows.
Work 1 row.
Cast off rem 26 sts.

SLEEVES
Using 3mm needles and A, cast on 56 sts.
Work 5cm K1, P1 rib, inc 4 sts evenly across last row. 60 sts.
Change to 4mm needles and work in patt as given for right front, inc 1 st at each end of 8 foll 12th rows in A only. 76 sts.
Work straight until sleeve measures 42cm from top of rib.
Shape top
Cast off 4 sts at beg of next 2 rows, then 2 sts at beg of foll 8 rows. Now dec 1 st at each end of foll 16 alt rows.
Cast off rem 20 sts.

MAKING UP
Join shoulder seams.
Neckband
Using 3mm needles and A, with RS of work facing, K up 84 sts around neck edge.
Work 2cm K1, P1 rib.
Cast off in rib.
Right front band
Using 3mm needles and A, with RS of work facing, K up 132 sts along right front opening and neckband.
Work 1cm K1, P1 rib, ending with a WS row.
Make buttonholes:
1st buttonhole row Rib 4, [cast off 3, rib 8 including st used to cast off] 11 times, cast off 3, rib to end.
2nd buttonhole row Rib to end, casting on 3 sts over those cast off in previous row.
Cont in rib until band measures 2cm.

Cast off in rib.
Make left front band in the same way omitting buttonholes.
Join side seams and sleeve seams.
Set in sleeves.
Sew on buttons.

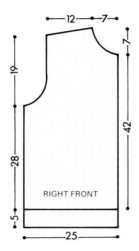

RIGHT FRONT

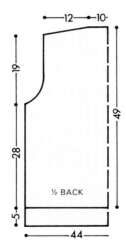

½ BACK

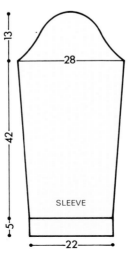

SLEEVE

Photograph: G. Bensimon   Designed by Simone Vassort

Laplander

Intricately patterned with traditional motifs, an ideal jacket for warding off Arctic chills.

SIZE
To fit 86–91cm bust

MATERIALS
650g double knitting yarn in main colour (A)
400g in 1st contrast colour (B)
50g in 2nd contrast colour (C)
1 pair each 2¾mm and 3¾mm needles
1 each 2¾mm and 3¾mm circular needles
8 buttons

TENSION
25 sts and 30 rows to 10cm over patt on 3¾mm needles.

BACK AND FRONTS (one piece)
Using 2¾mm circular needle and A, cast on 241 sts. Work 2cm K1, P1 rib in rows, ending with a WS row.
Make buttonhole:
1st buttonhole row Rib 2, cast off 3 sts, rib to end.

Chart 1

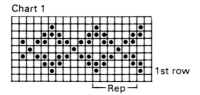

└─ Rep ─┘   1st row

Chart 2

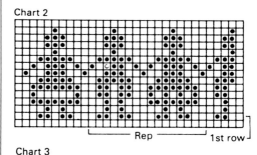

└──── Rep ────┘   1st row

Chart 3

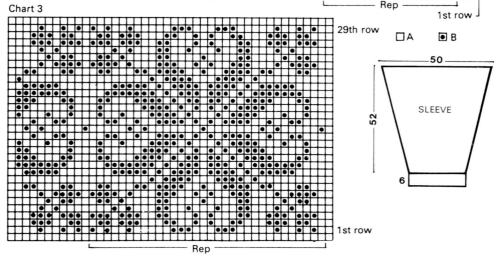

└──────── Rep ────────┘   1st row

2nd buttonhole row Rib to end, cast on 3 sts over those cast off in previous row.
Cont in rib until work measures 4cm from beg, ending with a RS row.
Next row Rib 9, leave these sts on a st holder for left front band, change to 3¾mm circular needle, inc 1 in next st, P to last 10 sts, inc 1 in next st, turn, leaving rem 9 sts on a st holder for right front band. 225 sts.
Work 3 rows st st, inc 32 sts evenly across 1st row. 257 sts.
Commence patt:
***Next row* (WS) [P1A, 1C] to last st, 1A.
Next row [K1C, 1A] to last st, 1C.**
Work 3 rows st st in A.***
Commence patt from chart 1:
1st row (RS) *K5A, 1B; rep from * to last 5 sts, 5A.
2nd row *P1B, 3A, 2B; rep from * to last 5 sts, 1B, 3A, 1B.
These 2 rows establish patt from chart 1, cont as set work 5 more rows from chart 1.
Work 4 rows st st in A.****
Rep from ** to ***.
Commence patt from chart 2:
1st row (RS)*K2A, 2B, 1A, 2B, 3A, [2B, 1A] twice; rep from * to last st, 1A.
2nd row *P3A, 1B, 1A, 1B, 5A, 1B, 1A, 1B, 2A; rep from * to last st, 1A.
These 2 rows establish patt from chart 2, cont as set work 11 more rows from chart.

Chart 4

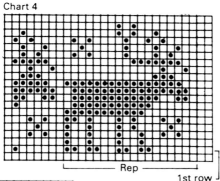

└──── Rep ────┘   1st row

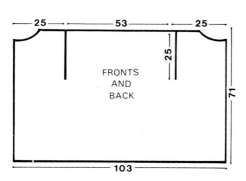

□ A   ◉ B

Work 4 rows st st in A.
Rep from ** to **** then from ** to *** again.
Commence patt from chart 3:
1st row (RS) *K[1A, 1B] twice, 2A, 1B, 5A, 3B, 3A, 3B, 5A, 1B, 2A, 1B, 1A, 1B; rep from * to last st, 1A.
2nd row P1A, *1A, 2B, 1A, 3B, 3A, 2B, 2A, 1B, 1A, 1B, 2A, 2B, 3A, 3B, 1A, 2B, 2A; rep from * to end.
These 2 rows establish patt from chart 3, cont as set work 3rd–29th rows from chart.
Work 4 rows st st in A.
Rep from ** to **** then from ** to **.
Divide for armholes
Next row With A, P64, leave these sts on a length of yarn for left front, P129, leave these sts on a length of yarn for back, P to end. 64 sts.
Cont on these sts only for right front.
Work 2 rows st st in A, inc 1 st at end of 1st row. 65 sts.
Commence patt from chart 4:
1st row (RS) K2A, [6A, 2B, 1A, 2B, 2A, 2B, 1A, 2B] 3 times, 9A.
2nd row P9A, [1B, 2A, 1B, 3A, 1B, 2A, 1B, 7A] 3 times, 2A.
These 2 rows establish position of reindeer motifs, cont as set working motifs from chart 4, work 16 more rows.
Work 3 rows st st in A.
Rep from ** to ****, then from ** to *** again.
Now work 1st–29th rows from chart 3 as set.*****
Next row With A, P to end.
Shape neck
Cont in st st, cast off 16 sts at beg of next row, then dec 1 st at neck edge on next 2 rows. 47 sts.
Rep from ** to ***, dec 1 st at neck edge on foll 2 alt rows. 45 sts.
Cast off.

29th row

1st row

50
52
SLEEVE
6

25 — 53 — 25
25
FRONTS AND BACK
71
103

Photograph: G. Lebaube   Designed by Kerstin Adolphson

Using 3¾mm needles and A, with RS facing rejoin yarn to sts left for left front. Work 2 rows st st, inc 1 st at beg of 1st row. 65 sts.
Commence patt reversing motif from chart 4:
1st row (RS) K9A, [2B, 1A, 2B, 2A, 2B, 1A, 2B, 6A] 3 times, 2A.
2nd row P2A, [7A, 1B, 2A, 1B, 3A, 1B, 2A, 1B] 3 times, 9A.
These 2 rows establish position of reversed reindeer motifs, cont as set reversing motifs from chart 4, work 16 more rows. Now complete to match right front reversing shaping.
Using 3¾mm needles and A, with RS of work facing rejoin yarn to sts left for back. Work 2 rows st st in A.
Commence patt, work 6 reindeer motifs from chart 4, reversing the 3 on RH side of back:
1st row (RS) K10A, [2B, 1A, 2B, 2A, 2B, 1A, 2B, 6A] 3 times, 1A, [6A, 2B, 1A, 2B, 2A, 2B, 1A, 2B] 3 times, 10A.
2nd row P10A, [1B, 2A, 1B, 3A, 1B, 2A, 1B, 7A] 3 times, 1A, [7A, 1B, 2A, 1B, 3A, 1B, 2A, 1B] 3 times, 10A.
These 2 rows establish the position of motifs, cont as set work 16 more rows from chart.
Cont as given for right front to *****.
Work 4 rows st st in A.
Rep from ** to ***. Cast off.

SLEEVES
Using 2¾mm needles and A, cast on 56 sts. Work 6cm K1, P1 rib, inc 9 sts evenly across last row. 65 sts.
Change to 3¾mm needles, cont in st st inc 1 st at each end of every foll 5th row until there are 125 sts, *at the same time* work chart patts in foll sequence:
Work 3 rows st st in A, beg with a K row.
Work as given for back from ** to ***.
Work patt from chart 2.
Work 4 rows st st in A.
Work as given for back from ** to ****, then from ** to *** again.
Work patt from chart 3.
Work 4 rows st st in A.
Work as given for back from ** to ****, then from ** to *** again.
Work reindeer motifs from chart 4, reversing the chart for left sleeve.
Work 3 rows st st in A.
Work as given for back from ** to ****, then from ** to *** again.
Cast off.

NECKBAND
Using 2¾mm needles and A, cast on 9 sts. Work in K1, P1 rib until band when slightly stretched fits round neck edge. Cast off in rib.

MAKING UP
Join shoulder seams.
Join sleeve seams and set in sleeves.
Join on neckband.
Left front band
Sl sts left for left front band on to 2¾mm needles, rejoin A and cont in K1, P1 rib until band when slightly stretched fits up entire left front edge. Cast off in rib.
Right front band
Mark positions for 7 buttons evenly spaced on left front band. Work right front band to match left, making buttonholes opposite markers.
Join on front bands. Sew on buttons.

Classic Chic

Stylish longline cardigan worked in traditional Aran trinity stitch, lozenge and cable patterns.

SIZES
To fit (86)91(96)cm bust

MATERIALS
(650)700(700)g double knitting yarn
1 pair each 3mm and 3¾mm needles
Cable needle
6 buttons

TENSION
32 sts and 30 rows to 10cm over patt A on 3¾mm needles.

SPECIAL ABBREVIATIONS
Cable 4 front — sl next 2 sts on to cable needle and hold at front of work, K2, then K2 from cable needle.
Cable 6 back — sl next 3 sts on to cable needle and hold at back of work, K3, then K3 from cable needle.
Cable 6 front — sl next 3 sts on to cable needle and hold at front of work, K3, then K3 from cable needle.
Cr2R (cross 2 right) — K 2nd st on LH needle, then P 1st st dropping both sts off needle at the same time.
Cr2L (cross 2 left) — sl next st on to cable needle and hold at front of work, P1, then K1 from cable needle.
5 from 1 — [K1, P1, K1, P1, K1] all into next st.

PANEL PATT A
Worked over (32)36(40) sts on back and fronts, and over (20)24(28) sts on sleeves.
1st row (RS) P.
2nd row *[K1, P1, K1] all into next st, P3 tog; rep from * to end.
3rd row P.
4th row *P3 tog, [K1, P1, K1] all into next st; rep from * to end.
Rep 1st–4th rows.

PANEL PATT B
Worked over 4 sts.
1st row (RS) K.
2nd row P.
3rd row Cable 4 front.
Rep 2nd–3rd rows.

PANEL PATT C
Worked over 18 sts.
1st row (RS) P3, K12, P3.
2nd row K3, P12, K3.
3rd row P3, cable 6 back, cable 6 front, P3.
4th row As 2nd row.
Rep 1st–4th rows.

PANEL PATT D
Worked over 13 sts on fronts, and over 37 sts on back and sleeves.
1st row (RS) [P5, sl next st on to cable needle and hold at front of work, Cr2R,

K1 from cable needle, P4] once for fronts (3 times for back and sleeves), P1.
2nd row [K5, P1, K1, P1, K4] once (3 times), K1.
3rd row [P4, Cr2R, P1, Cr2L, P3] once (3 times), P1.
4th row [K4, P1, K3, P1, K3] once (3 times), K1.
5th row [P3, Cr2R, P1, 5 from 1, P1, Cr2L, P2] once (3 times), P1.
6th row [K3, P1, K9, P1, K2] once (3 times), K1.
7th row [P2, Cr2R, P2, P5 tog, P2, Cr2L, P1] once (3 times), P1.
8th row [K2, P1, K7, P1, K1] once (3 times) K1.
9th row [P1, Cr2R, P1, 5 from 1, P3, 5 from 1, P1, Cr2L] once (3 times) P1.
10th row [K1, P1, K17, P1], once (3 times), K1.
11th row [P1, Cr2L, P1, P5 tog, P3, P5 tog, P1, Cr2R] once (3 times), P1.
12th row [K2, P1, K7, P1, K1] once (3 times), K1.
13th row [P2, Cr2L, P2, 5 from 1, P2, Cr2R, P1] once (3 times), P1.
14th row [K3, P1, K9, P1, K2] once (3 times), K1.
15th row [P3, Cr2L, P1, P5 tog, P1, Cr2R, P2] once (3 times), P1.
16th row [K4, P1, K3, P1, K3] once (3 times), K1.
17th row [P4, Cr2L, P1, Cr2R, P3] once (3 times), P1.
18th row [K5, P1, K1, P1, K4] once (3 times), K1.
Rep 1st–18th rows.

BACK
Using 3mm needles, cast on (138)146(154) sts.
Work 22cm K2, P2 rib.
Next row Rib (32)36(40), pick up loop between last st and next st and K it tbl to make 1, rib 2, make 1, rib 3, [make 1, rib 4] 16 times, make 1, rib 3, make 1, rib 2, make 1, rib (32)36(40). (159)167(175) sts.
Change to 3¾mm needles and commence patt:
1st row (RS) K1, work 1st row patt A, P2, 1st row patt B, 1st row patt C, 1st row patt B, 1st row patt D, 1st row patt B, 1st row patt C, 1st row patt B, P2, 1st row patt A, K1.
2nd row K1, work 2nd row patt A, K2, 2nd row patt B, 2nd row patt C, 2nd row patt B, 2nd row patt D, 2nd row patt B, 2nd row patt C, 2nd row patt B, K2, 2nd row patt A, K1.
These 2 rows establish the position of panel patts.
Cont as set, working first and last sts of every row as K sts, and 2 sts each side of

central panel of D in rev st st, until work measures (26)27(28)cm from top of rib, ending with a WS row.
Shape armholes
Cast off 15 sts at beg of next 2 rows. (129)137(145) sts.
Next row K1, P1, patt to last 2 sts, P1, K1.
Next row K2, patt to last 2 sts, K2.
Rep last 2 rows until armhole measures (19)20(21)cm from beg.
Shape shoulders
Cast off 10 sts at beg of next 2 rows. (109)117(125) sts.
Divide for neck
Next row Cast off (11)12(13) sts, patt (22)24(26) sts including st used to cast off, turn, leaving rem sts on a spare needle and cont on these sts only for right side of neck.
Next row Patt to end.
Next row Cast off (11)12(13) sts, patt to end. (11)12(13) sts.
Work 1 row. Cast off.
Return to sts on spare needle, with RS of work facing, rejoin yarn to next st, cast off (43)45(47) sts, patt to end. (33)36(39) sts.
Cast off (11)12(13) sts at beg of next and foll alt row.
Work 1 row.
Cast off rem (11)12(13) sts.

RIGHT FRONT
Using 3mm needles, cast on (67)71(75) sts.
Work 22cm K2, P2 rib.
Next row Rib 2, make 1, [rib 3, make 1] 11 times, rib to last st, make 1, rib 1. (80)84(88) sts.
Change to 3¾mm needles and commence patt:
1st row (RS) K1, P1, work 1st row patt B, 1st row patt D, 1st row patt B, 1st row patt C, 1st row patt B, P2, 1st row patt A, K1.
2nd row K1, work 2nd row patt A, K2, 2nd row patt B, 2nd row patt C, 2nd row patt B, 2nd row patt D, 2nd row patt B, K2.
These 2 rows establish the position of panel patts.
Cont as set, working first and last sts of every row as K sts, and 2nd st on RH edge and 2 sts on RH side of patt A in rev st st throughout, until right front measures (26)27(28)cm from top of rib, ending with a RS row.
Shape armhole and neck
Next row Cast off 15 sts, patt to last 2 sts, K2 tog.
Next row Patt to last 2 sts, P1, K1.
Next row K2, patt to last 2 sts, K2 tog. (63)67(71) sts.
Rep last 2 rows 16 times more. (47)51(55) sts.

Photograph: C. Duffy Designed by Alain Derda for Pingouin

Now, keeping armhole edge straight as set, dec 1 st at neck edge on next and foll (3)4(5) alt rows. (43)46(49) sts.
Work straight until armhole measures (19)20(21)cm, ending at armhole edge.
Shape shoulder
Cast off 10 sts at beg of next row and (11)12(13) sts at beg of foll 2 alt rows.
Work 1 row.
Cast off rem (11)12(13) sts.

LEFT FRONT
Using 3mm needles, cast on (67)71(75) sts.
Work 22cm K2, P2 rib.
Next row Rib 1, make 1, rib (31)35(39), [make 1, rib 3] 11 times, make 1, rib 2. (80)84(88) sts.
Change to 3¾mm needles and commence patt:
1st row (RS) K1, work 1st row patt A, P2, 1st row patt B, 1st row patt C, 1st row patt B, 1st row patt D, 1st row patt B, P1, K1.
2nd row K2, work 2nd row patt B, 2nd row patt D, 2nd row patt B, 2nd row patt C, 2nd row patt B, K2, 2nd row patt A, K1.
These 2 rows establish the position of panel patts.
Cont as set, working first and last sts of every row as K sts, and 2nd st on LH side and 2 sts on LH side of patt A in rev st st throughout.
Complete to match right front reversing all shapings.

SLEEVES
Using 3mm needles, cast on (54)58(62) sts.
Work 6cm K2, P2 rib, inc (35)39(43) sts evenly across last row. (89)97(105) sts.
Change to 3¾mm needles and commence patt:
1st row (RS) Work 1st row patt A, P2, 1st row patt B, 1st row patt D, 1st row patt B, P2, 1st row patt A.

2nd row Work 2nd row patt A, K2, 2nd row patt B, 2nd row patt D, 2nd row patt B, K2, 2nd row patt A.
These 2 rows establish position of panel patts.
Cont as set working 2 sts on each side of central panel in rev st st throughout at the same time inc and work into patt A 1 st at each end of 10th and every foll 11th row until there are (107)115(123) sts.
Work straight until sleeve measures (35)36(37)cm from top of rib, now inc 1 st at each end of every alt row until there are (113)121(129) sts.
Work straight until sleeve measures (41)42(43)cm from top of rib.
Cast off.

POCKETS (make 2)
Using 3mm needles, cast on 48 sts.
Work 15cm K2, P2 rib.
Cast off in rib.

NECK AND FRONT BAND
Using 3mm needles, cast on 13 sts.
Work 5cm K1, P1 rib.
Make buttonhole:
1st buttonhole row (RS) Rib 5, cast off 4 sts, rib to end.
2nd buttonhole row Rib to end, cast on 4 sts over those cast off in previous row.
Cont in rib making 5 more buttonholes at 8cm intervals until border is long enough when slightly stretched to fit round right front opening edge, back neck and left front opening edge.
Cast off in rib.

MAKING UP
Join shoulder seams.
Set sleeves in flat. Join side and sleeve seams.
Sew pockets on front welts matching ribs.
Join on neck and front band.
Sew on buttons.

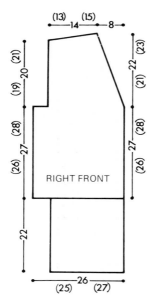

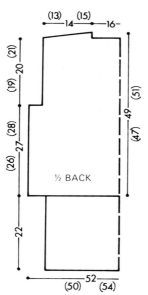

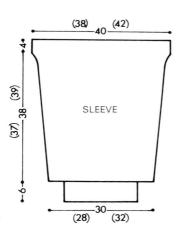

Redcoat

**A huge tree-of-life motif grows up
the back of this magnificent coat.
The pattern employs various
cross-over stitches but these are
easily worked from the charts.**

SIZE
To fit 86–91cm bust

MATERIALS
2100g extra-chunky yarn or chunky yarn
used double
1 pair 10mm needles
1 10.00mm crochet hook
Cable needle

TENSION
8½ sts and 12 rows to 10cm over st st on
10mm needles.

RIGHT FRONT
Cast on 30 sts.
Work from chart 1, working first 4 rows
in moss st then the first 2 patt rows thus:
1st row (RS) [K1, P1] 3 times, K4, P8, K2,
P6, [K1, P1] twice.
2nd row [P1, K1] twice, K6, P2, K8, P4,
[P1, K1] 3 times.
Cont working from chart, work 3rd–95th
rows.
Shape armhole
96th row Cast off 4 sts, patt to end from
chart. 26 sts.
Work 97th–118th rows.
Next row [K1, P1] 3 times, K2, P2, sl
these 10 sts on a st holder for neck and
cast off rem 16 sts.

key

☐ K on RS rows, P on WS rows

☑ P on RS rows, K on WS rows

sl next 2 sts on to cable needle and hold
at front of work, P2, then K2 from cable
needle

sl next 2 sts on to cable needle and hold
at front of work, [K1, yfwd, K1 tbl] all into
next st, P1, then K2 from cable needle

③ K3 on RS rows, P3 on WS rows

P3 tog

sl next st on to cable needle and hold at
front of work, K2, then K1 from cable
needle

sl next 2 sts on to cable needle and hold
at back of work, K2, then P first st from
cable needle and [K1, yfwd, K1 tbl] all into
second st on cable needle

sl next 2 sts on to cable needle and hold at
back of work, K2, then P2 from cable
needle

sl next 2 sts on to cable needle and hold at
back of work, K1, then K2 from cable
needle

sl next 2 sts on to cable needle and hold at
back of work, K1, then K1, P1 from cable
needle

sl next st on to cable needle and hold at
front of work, P1, K1, then K1 from cable
needle

[K1, yfwd, K1 tbl] all into next st

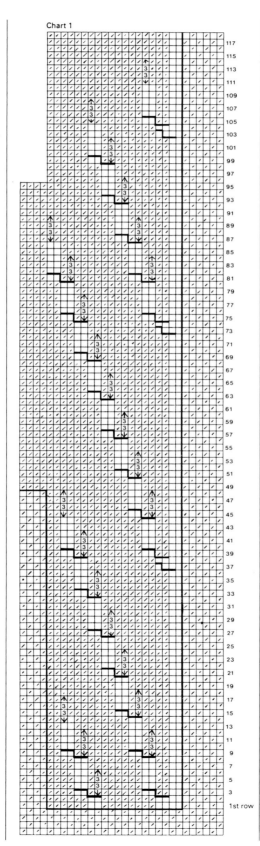

Chart 1

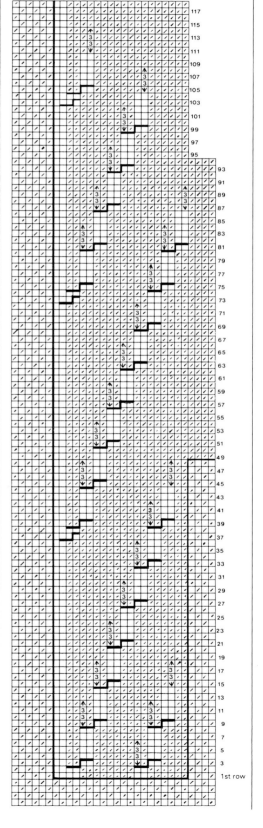

Chart 2

LEFT FRONT

Cast on 30 sts and work from chart 2 on page 107, working 4 rows moss st, then 1st–94th patt rows.

Shape armhole

95th row Cast off 4 sts, patt to end from chart. 26 sts.

Work 96th–118th rows from chart.

Next row Cast off 16 sts, P2 including st used to cast off, K2, [P1, K1] 3 times.

Sl rem 10 sts on to st holder.

BACK

Cast on 55 sts and work from chart 3, working 4 rows moss st, then 1st–94th patt rows.

Shape armholes

Patt next 2 rows from chart casting off 4 sts at beg of each row. 47 sts.

Work 97th–116th rows from chart.

Divide for neck

Next row P16, turn, leaving rem sts on spare needle, cont on these sts only for right side of neck.

Next row K to end.

Cast off.

Return to sts on spare needle, with RS of work facing rejoin yarn to next st, cast off 15 sts and complete to match right side of neck.

key

☐ K on RS rows, P on WS rows

☑ P on RS rows, K on WS rows

sl next 2 sts on to cable needle and hold at front of work, P2, then K2 from cable needle

sl next 2 sts on to cable needle and hold at front of work, [K1, yfwd, K1 tbl] all into next st, P1, then K2 from cable needle

③ K3 on RS rows, P3 on WS rows

P3 tog

sl next st on to cable needle and hold at front of work, K2, then K1 from cable needle

sl next 2 sts on to cable needle and hold at back of work, K2, then P first st from cable needle and [K1, yfwd, K1 tbl] all into second st on cable needle

sl next 2 sts on to cable needle and hold at back of work, K2, then P2 from cable needle

sl next 2 sts on to cable needle and hold at back of work, K1, then K2 from cable needle

sl next 2 sts on to cable needle and hold at back of work, K1, then K1, P1 from cable needle

sl next st on to cable needle and hold at front of work, P1, K1, then K1 from cable needle

[K1, yfwd, K1 tbl] all into next st

Chart 3

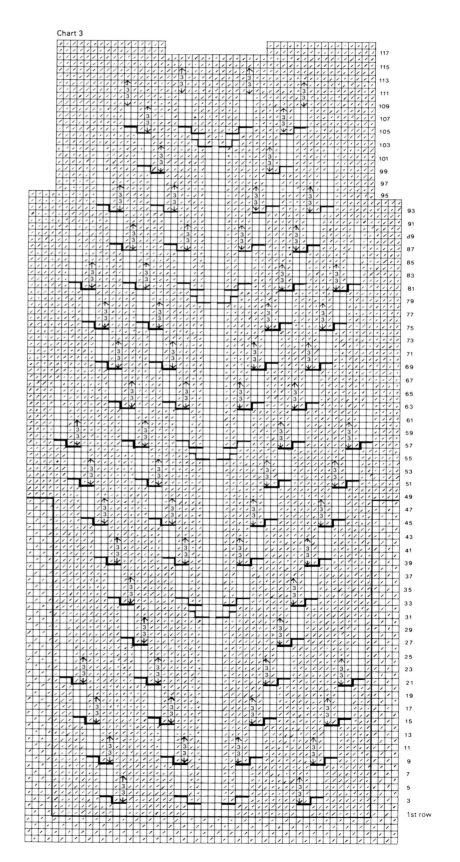

Photograph: J.-P. Metayer   Designed by Torrente

Redcoat

SLEEVES

Cast on 42 sts and work from chart 4 for right sleeve and chart 5 for left sleeve.
Work 1st–52nd rows.
Cast off.

MAKING UP

Join shoulder seams. Set sleeves in flat.
Join underarm seams.
Using 10.00mm crochet hook, join side seams from 35th patt row to armhole with a row of double crochet worked from the right side of the work and through both thicknesses.

Collar

With RS of work facing, K 10 sts from st holder at right front neck, K up 16 sts from back neck, K 10 sts from left front st holder. 36 sts.
Work 8 rows moss st.
Cast off in patt.
Work a row of double crochet down both sides of front opening, along lower edge of coat including side slits and edges of both sleeves.
Fold back cuffs.

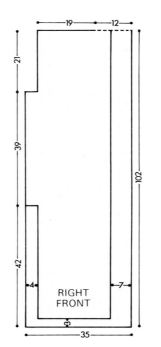

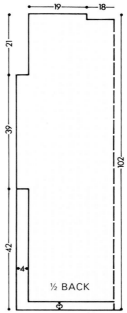

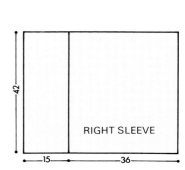

Chart 4

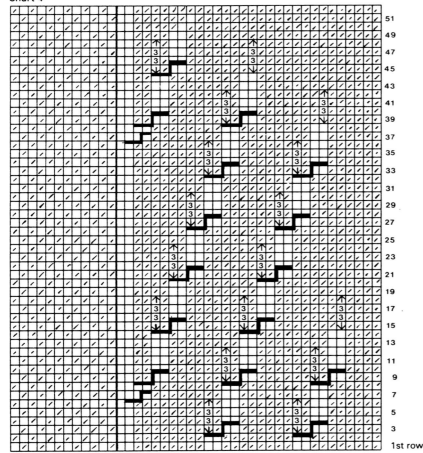

key

☐ K on RS rows, P on WS rows

☑ P on RS rows, K on WS rows

③ K3 on RS rows, P3 on WS rows

Ⓝ P3 tog

sl next 2 sts on to cable needle and hold at back of work, K2, then P first st from cable needle and [K1, yfwd, K1 tbl] all into second st on cable needle

sl next 2 sts on to cable needle and hold at back of work, K2, then P2 from cable needle

sl next 2 sts on to cable needle and hold at back of work, K1, then K2 from cable needle

sl next 2 sts on to cable needle and hold at back of work, K1, then K1, P1 from cable needle

[K1, yfwd, K1 tbl] all into next st

Redcoat

Chart 5

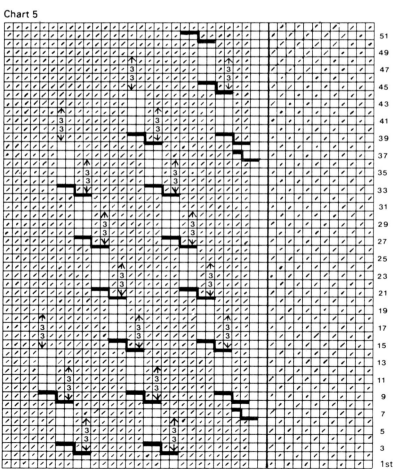

key

□ K on RS rows, P on WS rows

☑ P on RS rows, K on WS rows

③ K3 on RS rows, P3 on WS rows

⚟ P3 tog

sl next 2 sts on to cable needle and hold at front of work, P2, then K2 from cable needle

sl next 2 sts on to cable needle and hold at front of work, [K1, yfwd, K1 tbl] all into next st, P1, then K2 from cable needle

sl next st on to cable needle and hold at front of work, K2, then K1 from cable needle

sl next st on to cable needle and hold at front of work, P1, K1, then K1 from cable needle

⬦ ⬇ [K1, yfwd, K1 tbl] all into next st

Equipment and Materials

One of the great advantages of knitting is that the equipment is simple, and the working materials are beautiful and varied.

THE NEEDLES

Knitting needles are the only really essential tools for all types of knitting. There are various kinds and most of them come in a range of sizes. In general, the thicker the yarn the larger the needle size used to work it. It is important to remember that the needle size quoted in a pattern is no more than a recommended size. It is intended to be used as a starting point for making tension samples. Many knitters will end up using a different size from the one specified.

TYPES OF NEEDLES

Single-pointed needles are the most common ones. They are sold in pairs and used for flat knitting. Nowadays they are usually made of a metal alloy but it is still possible to get plastic ones and many knitters find these more comfortable. As well as a full range of thicknesses they come in several lengths. Before beginning on a pattern, check whether it involves a large number of stitches. If it does, buy the longest needles.

Double-pointed needles come in sets of four or five and are used for knitting in the round. They come in a full range of thicknesses and several lengths. They can also be used for flat knitting so if a pattern lists a pair and a set of the same size needles, it may be possible to use two of the set instead of a pair.

Circular needles are sold singly. Each one consists of a pair of short pointed rods joined by a length of flexible wire. They come in a range of thicknesses and lengths and are used for knitting in the round, or for flat knitting where an exceptionally large number of stitches is involved.

Cable needles are used for working cable stitch patterns. They are short and double-pointed. Some are straight; others have a small kink or bend in the middle to help keep the stitches safely on the needle. They come in two thicknesses. Use the thinner ones with fine yarns and the thicker one with chunkier yarns. If a cable needle is needed for a particular pattern it will be listed along with the rest of the materials.

ACCESSORIES

Apart from the needles there are some other gadgets which will come in useful.
Stitch holders are rather like large safety pins and are used to hold stitches in waiting until they are needed at a later stage in the pattern. A spare needle or length of yarn will usually do the job just as well. For very small numbers of stitches an actual safety pin is ideal.

Row counters can be slotted on to the ends of single-pointed needles. They can help the knitter keep track of complicated stitch patterns.

Stitch stoppers are rubber or plastic guards that can be pushed onto the points of needles to prevent the stitches slipping off and unravelling.

Needle gauges are metal plates pierced with holes corresponding to international needle sizes. These are useful for measuring the size of needles, like circular and double-pointed needles, that are not marked with their size.

Wool needles are sewing needles specially designed for sewing up knitted garments. They have rounded points that will not split the stitches.

Other items in general use that will be needed are a pair of sharp scissors, pins, a tape measure for taking body measurements and a rigid ruler for measuring the knitting itself.

NEEDLE SIZES

Metric	UK	US	Metric	UK	US
2mm	14	00	5mm	6	7
2¼mm	13	0	5½mm	5	8
2½mm	—	—	6mm	4	9
2¾mm	12	1	6½mm	3	10
3mm	11	2	7mm	2	10½
3¼mm	10	3	7½mm	1	11
3½mm	—	—	8mm	0	12
3¾mm	9	4	9mm	00	13
4mm	8	5	10mm	000	15
4½mm	7	6			

THE YARNS

At one time 'yarn' was virtually synonymous with 'wool'. Now the range of yarns available to the knitter is bewilderingly wide and growing every year. Yarns made from some of the less common natural fibres – silk and linen, for example – are becoming more accessible in a wider selection of colours and finishes than ever before, and there are hundreds of new synthetic yarns of variable quality and properties, as well as novelty yarns and fancy threads which change with every season.

NATURAL FIBRES

Many knitters prefer to work only with natural fibres.
Wool, spun from sheep's fleece, is the most important of these. The best wool is 'pure new wool' which signifies that it has not previously been processed in any way. The best 'pure new wool' is often marked with the Woolmark, the symbol devised by the International Wool Secretariat to mark wool which reaches high standards in its class.

There are many different types of wool, its quality depending on the age and breed of the sheep as well as on the processing. Botany wool, which comes exclusively from merino sheep, is the softest, warmest type. Lambswool, also very fine and soft, comes from the 'first clip' of the young animal's fleece. Less soft, but very much stronger is the wool spun from semi-wild Cumbrian Herdwick sheep and from Jacob's sheep. These are usually only available in their natural colours – cream, through browns and greys to black. Shetland wool or 'fingering', spun from sheep raised in the Shetland Isles, is loosely twisted, light and warm. It is available in a range of colours and is especially suitable for traditional Shetland and Fair Isle patterns. In addition, there are highly specialised wools like the finest Shetland laceweight yarn handspun from wool plucked from the neck and back of the sheep, and 'bainin', the creamy coloured hardwearing yarn used for traditional Aran knitting. There is also a special tightly twisted wool made for knitting classic Guernseys. Wool of all types is the archetypal knitting yarn. It has all the desirable qualities – softness, warmth, strength and elasticity. It takes and holds dyes well and it's a sympathetic fibre to work with.

Mohair is another very popular yarn of animal origin. Spun from the hair of the Ankara goat, it is an unusually strong and hardwearing yarn which has the useful property of resisting dirt particles. However, the long fibres which account for its attractive, fluffy, slightly shiny appearance can irritate sensitive skin and it is rarely suitable for baby or children's clothes especially in its pure form. For this reason, and for reasons of cost, it is often found mixed with other softer and cheaper fibres, natural or synthetic.

Cashmere is another expensive goat hair yarn. The hairs are combed from Kashmiri goats in their moulting season and are especially light and soft. Though very comfortable to knit, it requires careful washing to avoid shrinkage.

Alpaca is an increasingly common fibre

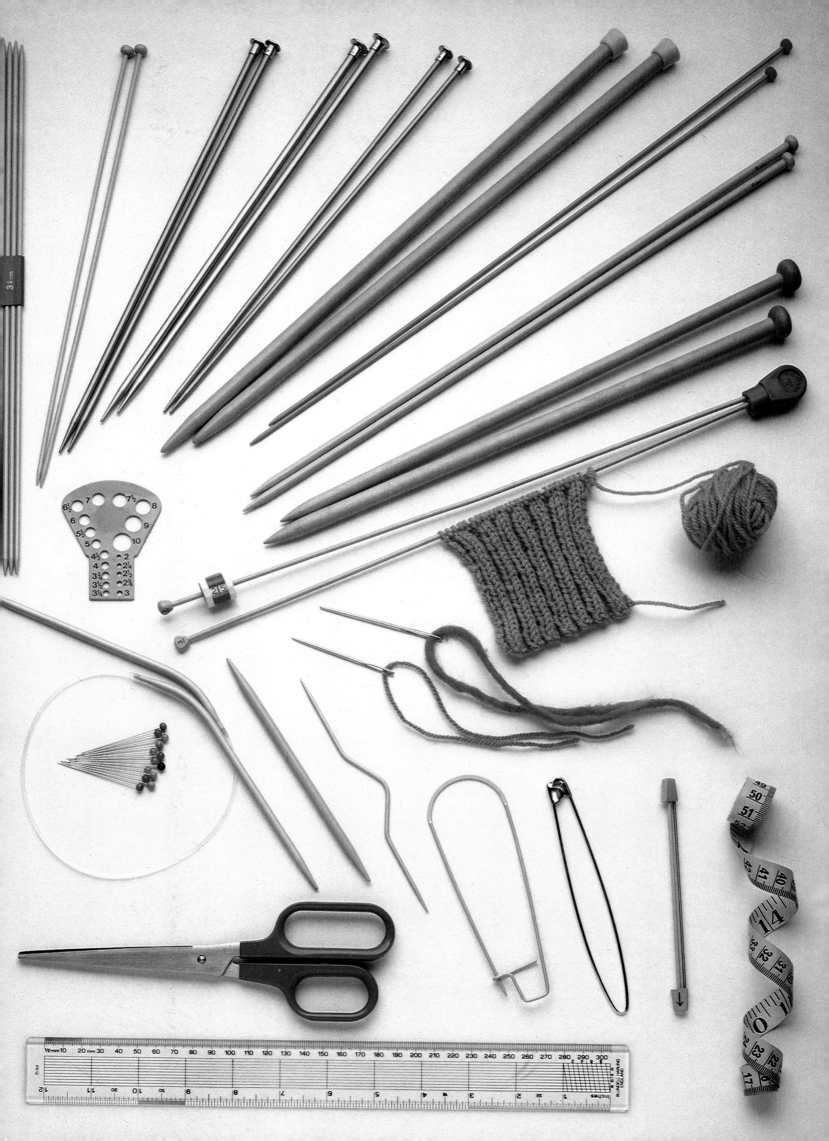

of South American origin which is found in its pure form and mixed with other fibres especially wool. In its more usual natural state the colour ranges from creamy to dark brownish black, but it is also sometimes dyed.

Angora is produced from the fine silky coat of the Angora rabbit. It is a luxurious yarn with a definite glossy sheen which dyes well to soft pastels and deep rich shades. Making up can be a problem as the yarn is so slippery. The finish is fluffy, even shaggy, but unlike mohair it does not irritate the skin. The main disadvantage of angora is the cost.

Silk, also of animal origin, is produced by silk worms, the larvae of the silk moth. There are several kinds used for knitting, from the very shiny reeled silk to coarser slubbier tussah. It is the strongest of all the natural fibres and can be rather difficult to handle being at once slippery and harsh. Often it is mixed with other fibres. Wool and silk is a particularly compatible combination.

Cotton, made from the seed pod of a member of the mallow family, is the most important fibre of plant origin. It is very strong and durable and has the advantage of being cool in summer and fairly warm in winter. It is resistent to moths and is easily dyed. There is very little elasticity in the fibres so it is less comfortable to knit with than wool. It needs careful washing and a long drying period.

Linen is made from the flax plant and is second in strength only to silk. Like cotton it is moth-resistent and easily dyed. It is an expensive yarn and is often found in mixtures especially with cotton.

SYNTHETIC FIBRES

Many types of synthetic fibre are used in the manufacture of knitting yarns including nylon (polyamides), polyesters and acrylics. There are also fibres which, though not technically synthetic, since they originate in natural fibres (like wood pulp and cotton waste), are 'man-made'. The most important of these are viscose and triacetate. Being regenerated fibres they tend to be rather weak but they have other qualities which make them useful (the shininess of viscose, for example).

Most synthetic yarns are designed to duplicate the advantages of natural fibres and avoid the disadvantages. This they do with varying amounts of success. They are usually shrink-proof (in water) and moth- and mildew-resistant. However, they are often subject to heat damage and drying and pressing can be a problem. Though they do not felt in the same way as wool, for example, there is often a tendency to

'pilling' where small balls of fibres form on the surface of the fabric, and to static electricity which affects not only the feel of a garment but also the hang and the colour. Generally they are most successful when mixed with other, natural fibres.

TYPES OF YARN

Apart from the fibre composition one of the main factors affecting the nature of yarn is the way in which the fibres are processed or spun. Both natural and synthetic fibres are available in a range of finishes. There are the smooth plain classic yarns, which can be loosely twisted like Shetland yarn, medium-twisted like most conventional knitting wools, or tightly twisted like crêpe yarns and Guernsey 5-ply. The tighter the twist, the more tough and hardwearing the yarn will be. Cottons also vary: they can be soft and matt, or mercerised which makes them harder and shinier. Some yarn finishes are designed to produce different textures in the knitted fabric. Bouclé and loop yarns produce crunchy curly textures. Slub and flake yarns result in a knobbly uneven fabric. Chenille has a velvety finish. Then there are innumerable novelty yarns that combine fibres and colours in many different ways or which simulate other threads like gold and silver, ribbon or leather thonging.

SIZING

Most yarns are made up of several single strands twisted together. These single strands are known as plies and some of the yarns made from them are referred to by the number of plies they contain. This is a guide, though not an infallible guide, to the size or thickness of the yarn.

One-ply yarn is a scarce extremely fine yarn used for knitting exceptionally fine delicate Shetland 'ring' shawls and of limited use for other purposes.

Two-ply yarn is also very fine, but the traditional Shetland wool which knits 'as four-ply' is also technically two-ply. When buying Shetland yarn for sweaters make sure it is the type described as 'jumper weight'.

Three-ply is a fine yarn used for making lightweight garments and baby clothes. Botany wool is often a three-ply yarn.

Four-ply is one of the most commonly used thicknesses. It is a fine lightweight yarn knitted on fairly small needles and particularly suitable for intricate colour-patterned garments like Fair Isle sweaters and cardigans and for lacy stitches. Many of the commoner fine cotton yarns also knit 'as four-ply'.

Double knitting is a very popular

medium-weight yarn. It knits up more quickly than four-ply but is still fairly light and therefore suitable for a wide range of garment types. It is often used for cable and textured stitches as well as colour patterns.

Aran-weight yarn is slightly thicker than double knitting and is used for outdoor garments as well as traditional Aran sweaters. Textured stitches show up particularly well in this weight.

Chunky yarn is another common type, thicker than Aran and used for heavy outdoor sweaters, jackets and coats. Some lighter but very loosely twisted bulky yarns (sometimes called *mèche* yarns) also 'knit as chunky'.

Many of the different fibres are available in all these thicknesses. Others are more limited. Cotton, for example, is rarely found thicker than double knitting and, for obvious reasons, the more expensive fibres like cashmere, alpaca and silk are not found in pure form in the heavier weights.

Key to yarns opposite
1 Random-dyed wool twisted with Lurex.
2 Space-dyed flake wool. 3 Undyed British Herdwick wool. 4 Undyed British Swaledale wool. 5 Fine glitter yarn. 6 Chunky Icelandic *mèche* wool. 7 Double knitting weight matt cotton. 8 Fine cashmere. 9 Double knitting weight mercerised cotton. 10 Five-ply Guernsey wool. 11 Fine soft cotton. 12 Wool and silk mixture. 13 Two-ply Shetland lace weight wool. 14 Pure silk. 15 Traditional Aran 'bainin' wool. 16 Dyed alpaca. 17 Chunky tweed wool. 18 Mohair. 19 Angora and lambswool mixture. 20 Two-ply Shetland jumper weight wool. 21 Cotton chenille.

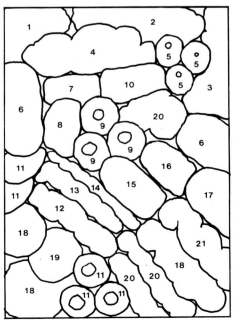

Choosing and Buying Yarn

**Finding a suitable yarn is the first
step towards making a successful
garment.**

In many cases the only choice available to
the knitter is that of colour since the type
and brand of yarn has been specified by
the publisher of the pattern. While this is
certainly the 'safest' course of action in
that the result will be a garment almost
identical to the one illustrated, it is also
unnecessarily restricting, particularly in
view of the many wonderful yarns on sale
nowadays.

In this book, only generic types of yarn
have been listed in the materials section
of each pattern. (For knitters who would
like to obtain the original yarns, these are
listed on page 126.) Yarns have been
described by their approximate size or
thickness – double knitting, Aran-weight,
four-ply and so on – and, while this system
has the advantage of flexibility and
greater individuality in the finished
garments, it does mean that the choice of
yarn for each pattern must be exercised
with much greater forethought and
caution than usual. In particular, it
means that the *quantities* given can only
be *estimates*. It is also essential to choose a
yarn that is suitable for its purpose in
terms of the type of garment and the
stitch pattern and, most important of all,
that will knit up to the required tension.

SUITABILITY

Out of the thousands of different yarns on
the market only a dozen or so may be
suitable for a particular garment. The
fibre composition is important to the
warmth, durability, cleaning
requirements and to the 'handle' of a
garment – whether it is soft or coarse to
the touch. Many people are unable to wear
certain rough fibres next to their skin
which means that many types of wool and
mohair are automatically excluded from
the choice. It is unwise to use any of the
hairier types of wool or mohair on
children's or baby clothes. Angora can be
positively harmful as children have been
known to choke on its loose slippery fibres.

The insulation properties of yarns vary
considerably. For greatest warmth choose
loosely twisted yarns with a high
percentage of wool or mohair in them.
Cashmere and angora are also noted for
warmth. The coolest fibres are cotton and
linen so choose these for summer
garments. Synthetics, silk and tightly
twisted yarns generally occupy the middle
range. Many styles of garment are
suitable for making in several different
types of yarn, producing garments totally
different in character from the same
pattern. The sweater on page 44, for
example, could be knitted in cotton for
summer or spring, a loosely twisted

TENSION CHART

Standard tension over stocking stitch using classic 100% wool yarns (number of stitches
and rows to 10cm).

Needle size (mm)	4-ply sts	rows	Double knit sts	rows	Aran sts	rows	Chunky sts	rows
2¾ mm	32	40	—	—	—	—	—	—
3mm	30	38	—	—	—	—	—	—
3¼mm	28	36	24	33	—	—	—	—
3¾mm	26	34	23	31	—	—	—	—
4mm	24	32	22	28	20	26	—	—
4½mm	—	—	21	26	19	24	—	—
5mm	—	—	20	25	18	22	—	—
5½mm	—	—	—	—	17	21	13	17
6mm	—	—	—	—	—	—	12	16

Shetland yarn for winter or, for evening wear, in a metallic novelty yarn.

Another factor in the suitability of the yarn for its purpose is the finish or texture. Not all yarns are suitable for all stitch patterns. Some, like heavy bouclé, loop or slub yarns, should only be used for plain simple stitches like stocking stitch and garter stitch. Lacy stitches and lightly textured stitches like basketweave and seed stitches would be totally obscured by such yarns. Most textured stitch patterns should be worked in plain smooth yarns. If the stitch is heavily embossed then lightly fluffy or flecked yarns can be effective. Delicate, fluffy yarns are particularly suitable for lacy patterns. Lace stitches usually also work well in cotton. Cables and crossover patterns show up best in fairly plain yarns, either smooth or brushed. Bold multi-coloured patterns (page 64, for example) can be worked in yarns with some surface texture such as light bouclé, mohair and slub yarns. More intricate patterns with small motifs are best in smooth yarns that display the fine detail of the pattern.

TENSION

Correct tension is the most important single factor in the success of any knitted garment. If the knitter does not match the tension specified in the pattern the garment will simply be too big or too small. (See page 120 for detailed information on measuring, checking and adjusting tension.) When choosing yarn it is essential to find one that can be knitted up to the tension given in the pattern. In virtually every case this will entail choosing a yarn in the same size group as that specified, but it does not mean that each and every double knitting yarn or four-ply yarn can be knitted up to the tension given for a particular double knitting or four-ply in a particular pattern. Yarns can vary a great deal as to tension even if they belong to the same group. The tension table given opposite is an average only. The actual figures can be as much as two or three stitches or rows more or less. The only sure way of finding out whether it is possible to achieve a particular tension with a particular yarn is to knit up a sample and measure it. Before you get to that stage however, there is often a good deal of information on yarn labels and ball bands that will help narrow the choice.

READING BALL BANDS

Most modern yarn labels are very informative. At their best they display the fibre content, washing and pressing symbols, shade number, dye lot number, weight of the ball in metric and imperial measures, length of thread also in metric and imperial measures and of course, the name of the manufacturer and the brand name of the yarn. The description of the yarn may include its thickness (double knitting, for example) or it may simply be a fanciful but relatively meaningless name. In any case, there may also be a recommended needle size and tension measurement. This is the tension which, in the manufacturer's view, produces the correct handle in the knitted fabric – neither so tight that the yarn is stretched

and damaged and the fabric stiff, nor so loose that it has little body or shape. If this measurement is near that given in the pattern then it is likely that the given tension can be achieved either on the same or a different needle size. When making the comparison check that both tensions are quoted over the same stitch pattern. On ball bands it is almost always stocking stitch.

The ball band is less helpful if, as often happens, the pattern designer has deliberately chosen to use a yarn at an unorthodox tension in order to achieve a specific effect. In this case there is no alternative to buying a ball of yarn and making up a sample. If, by sampling or checking the ball band, it is impossible to achieve the correct row and stitch tension, choose a yarn that will give you the correct stitch tension and adjust the length by working more or fewer rows.

QUANTITY

Having found a yarn which has a suitable fibre composition and finish, and which will knit up to the correct tension the only remaining problem is that of quantity. How much of this yarn will it take to complete the garment. Each pattern lists an amount of yarn, but this is only an approximation based on the amount of the original yarn that was required. You may need more or less of the new yarn, especially if the fibre content or finish is different.

The amount of yarn needed to complete a garment is directly related to the length of the thread. However, yarn is sold by weight and the length of yarn per 50g ball varies according to the thickness of the yarn, its fibre content and finish. The 'heaviest' yarns are cotton and linen, followed by wool, mohair and, finally, the lightest yarns, the synthetics. There is more length for the same weight in wholly synthetic yarns and, for this reason, they are said to 'go further'. The length of the thread is also affected by the finish. A tightly twisted yarn has less length per 50g ball than a loosely twisted yarn made of the same fibres and novelty yarns with

a lot of extra curls, knobbles and slubs are relatively heavier than smooth yarns so you will need relatively more of these.

ESTIMATING QUANTITY

The only sure way of knowing the exact amount needed for a specific garment is to knit it up, by which time it is too late to find that you haven't enough. A reasonable estimate can be made by knitting up a single ball in the correct stitch pattern and tension and using that as a basis for calculating the remaining amount. Divide the total area of the garment (worked out from the measurement diagram) by the area that can be knitted with one ball to give you the total number of balls needed.

In practice, when buying yarn it is often possible to obtain advice from the shop itself on the amount needed for a particular garment. Specialist shops are also usually quite willing to reserve yarn against the possibility that it will be needed later. If you have to buy it all at once, the table given below should give you some guidance. Use it together with the information on the ball band and with the estimate given in the pattern. If in doubt always buy more than you think you will need. Any left over can be used for repair jobs or for knitting stitch samples.

DYE LOT

Make sure that all the yarn you buy comes from the same dye lot as there is a remarkable amount of difference between them even in 'no-colour' colours like black and white. While this may not be seen when the yarn is in the ball it becomes glaringly obvious when it is knitted up.

Approximate yarn requirement for a long-sleeved round-necked sweater, size 91cm bust or chest, knitted in stocking stitch.

Yarn thickness	Fibre content	Number of 50g balls
3-ply	100% cotton	10
	100% wool	7
	75% acrylic/25% wool	7
4-ply	100% cotton	11
	100% wool	8
	75% acrylic/25% wool	7
	100% acrylic	6
Double knitting	100% cotton	13
	50% wool/50% silk	10
	100% wool	9
	75% acrylic/25% wool	8
	70% mohair/30% acrylic	8
Aran	100% wool	12
	75% acrylic/25% wool	10
	60% acrylic/40% mohair	8
Chunky	100% wool	16
	75% acrylic/25% wool	14
	60% acrylic/40% mohair	12

Reading the Patterns

**To the uninitiated the language of
knitting patterns is meaningless
but after a while it's easy to find
your way about.**

All knitting patterns contain the same
kinds of information but the way that
information is conveyed can vary.
Differences of punctuation, abbreviation
and the way charts, for example, are laid
out can be confusing. This section is
specifically intended to help you read the
patterns in this book, but some of it will
also be helpful with other patterns.

All knitting patterns should contain the
following types of information: the size of
the finished garment, a list of the
materials and equipment required to
make it, a tension measurement, a key to
the abbreviations used, a set of working
instructions for each part of the garment,
which may include charts as well as
written instructions, and finally a guide to
making up and finishing the garment. In
most cases there will also be a sketch or
photograph of the garment. In this book
there is also a star rating which will give
the knitter some idea of the level of
difficulty involved in the pattern. This is
explained on page 7.

SIZE
Most of the patterns in this book provide
instructions for several sizes. The
instructions for the different sizes are
separated by round brackets. The first
section of each pattern indicates what
sizes are provided for and how those sizes
are to be displayed. For example, where,
as in most instances, there are three sizes,
the first size is given inside round
brackets, followed by the second size
outside brackets and then the third size
inside another set of round brackets thus:
(1st size)2nd size(3rd size). This means
that where in the pattern there is a set of
instructions given in similar formation,
the instructions in the first set of brackets
must be followed for the 1st size, those
without the brackets for the second size
and those in the second set of brackets for
the 3rd size. Where there are no brackets
the instructions are the same for all sizes.

The sizes quoted in this section are
always 'to fit' sizes, given in terms of a
bust or chest measurement for adults and
an age for children. The 'to fit'
measurement includes an allowance for
ease of movement or tolerance in the
garment which can range from a small
amount for a close-fitting garment to
quite a lot for something loose and baggy.
The actual measurements of the finished
garment are given on a measurement
diagram like the one on the right or, in
the case of garments knitted in the round,
under the 'to fit' measurement. When
deciding which size to knit, look at the
actual measurements as well as the to fit

measurement. You may well decide to
knit a larger or smaller size than the one
that is notionally to fit. The measurement
diagram will also help you discover
whether you need to make any
adjustments to the pattern, either before
you begin or during the course of the
work. This check on the actual
measurements is particularly important
in the case of children's clothes where the
to fit measurement is in terms of age only.

MATERIALS
The list of materials includes the yarn,
size and type of needles, including cable
needles, and anything else in the way of
buttons, zips or trimmings needed to
complete that particular garment. It does
not include all the ancillary items that are
always needed like tape measure, scissors,
stitch holders and sewing up needles. In
this book the patterns specify general
types of yarn rather than specific brands
so the quantities given can only be
approximate. Read the information on
pages 116–17 before buying the yarn.
Remember also that the needle sizes given
in these (and any other) patterns are also
estimated, since the size you should
actually use is dependent on your tension
check (see page 120).

Where more than one colour or type of
yarn is used these are coded A, B, C and so
on in the list of materials. These codes will
be used throughout the instructions.
Where a great many colours are used it
can be helpful to mark each ball with the
relevant code to avoid confusion.

TENSION
It is vital to check your tension before
embarking on the pattern. The procedure
for this is given in detail on page 120.

ABBREVIATIONS
All knitting patterns are written in
abbreviated form in order to save space
and avoid much tedious repetition. The
abbreviations used in this book are listed
on page 7. With some patterns there is
also a list of special abbreviations that are
relevant only to that pattern. Where, in
the course of the pattern, there is an
instruction to 'inc' or 'dec' a certain
number of stitches without any further
detail, any appropriate method of
increasing or decreasing may be used.

WORKING INSTRUCTIONS
Unless the garment is made in one piece
the working instructions are usually
divided up under appropriate headings for
the separate pieces – back, front, sleeves
and so on. These correspond to the
sections shown in the measurement
diagram. Work them in the order in which
they are printed since the instructions for
any stitch pattern used are often fully laid
out only in the first section. Thereafter it
will simply be referred to as 'patt'. Where
several different stitch patterns are
arranged in vertical panels on a garment,
these patterns may be laid out quite
separately before the actual working
instructions for each section begin. They
are referred to as panel patterns and are a
means of simplifying what would
otherwise be very lengthy instructions. It
can be helpful to familiarise yourself with
panel patterns by making samples before
beginning work on the garment itself.
Otherwise they can be ignored until you
are instructed to refer to them during the
course of the work.

Read right through the working
instructions before you begin. Make sure
that you understand the meaning of all

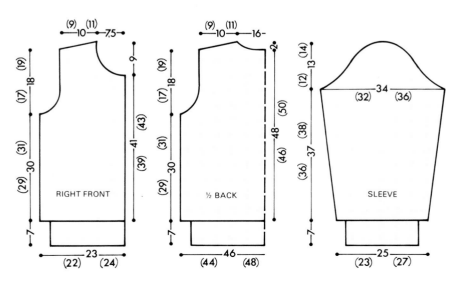

the abbreviations used in the pattern and that you are familiar with the basic stitches whose instructions are not given in detail. It is assumed that most knitters know how to work stocking stitch, garter stitch, reverse stocking stitch and K1, P1 and K2, P2 rib. Those who do not should read the instructions on page 121.

All knitting patterns involve repeats. It may be necessary to repeat a sequence of stitches during a row, or a sequence of rows, or shaping instructions, or whole sections of a pattern. These repeats are signalled in a variety of ways. In this book, repeats are marked by asterisks or square brackets. The use of asterisks is self-explanatory ('rep from * to end of row' or 'rep from ** to **' for example). In the case of square brackets, the instruction inside the brackets should be repeated the number of times stated immediately after the brackets (for example, '[K2 tog] 8 times'). Where there is a sequence of instructions inside the brackets the whole sequence should be repeated the stated number of times (for example, '[K1, P3, K4] 8 times').

CHARTS

Two types of chart can appear as part of the working instructions – stitch pattern charts and colourwork charts. In theory the whole of a knitting pattern can be charted though, in this book, only the pattern on page 101 falls into that category. Both stitch and colourwork charts are in the form of a grid where one stitch is represented by one square, and a row of stitches by a row of squares. All the charts are worked from the bottom upwards. The first row to be worked is usually the bottom row of the chart and is always marked as '1st row'. A chart may

represent a motif to be worked only once on a section of the garment, or it may represent a pattern to be repeated either horizontally or vertically or both. In any case, the written instructions will inform you where to place the charted motif or pattern. In some cases the first few rows of the chart will also be written out in full, in others you may be instructed to work from one point on the chart to another.

The same chart can be used for flat and circular knitting though it will be read differently. For flat knitting, read right-side rows from right to left and wrong-side rows from left to right. In circular knitting, every row on the chart represents a round of knitting and all rows must be read from right to left. Unless otherwise indicated, all colourwork charts should be worked in stocking stitch.

All charts are accompanied by a key that explains the meaning of the symbols used in the chart. Each symbol refers either to the type of stitch that should be worked or to the colour that should be used for the stitch. In some cases it refers to both. The colour codes used in the key are those used in the list of materials.

MAKING UP

This section describes how to put together the various pattern pieces and is described in full on pages 122–23.

NOTES FOR US KNITTERS

American knitters will have few problems in working from English patterns and *vice versa*. The main difficulties arise from some differences in terminology and the fact that knitting in the UK has become entirely metricated. The following charts should prove useful. American needle sizes are listed alongside their old English and metric equivalents in the table on page 112.

TERMINOLOGY

UK	US
cast off	bind off
double crochet	single crochet
stocking stitch	stockinette stitch
Swiss darning	duplicate stitch
tension	gauge
yarn forward	yarn over

All other terms are the same in both countries.

METRIC CONVERSION TABLES

Length (to the nearest ¼in)		Weight (rounded up to the nearest ¼oz)	
cm	in	g	oz
1	½	25	1
2	¾	50	2
3	1¼	100	3¾
4	1½	150	5½
5	2	200	7¼
6	2½	250	9
7	2¾	300	10¾
8	3	350	12½
9	3½	400	14¼
10	4	450	16
11	4¼	500	17¾
12	4¾	550	19½
13	5	600	21¼
14	5½	650	23
15	6	700	24¾
16	6¼	750	26½
17	6¾	800	28¼
18	7	850	30
19	7½	900	31¾
20	8	950	33¾
25	9¾	1000	35½
30	11¾		
35	13¾		
40	15¾		
45	17¾		
50	19¾		
55	21¾		
60	23½		
65	25½		
70	27½		
75	29½		
80	31½		
85	33½		
90	35½		
95	37½		
100	39½		

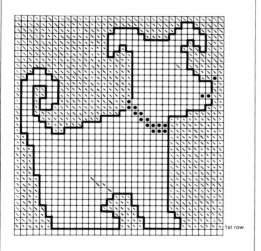

1st row

● P   □ K

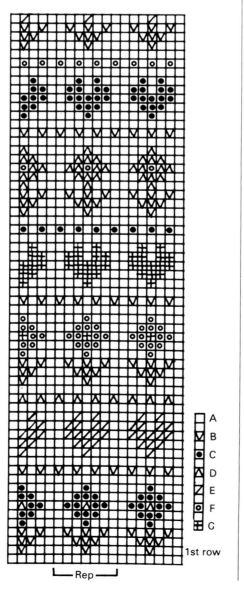

A
B
C
D
E
F
G

1st row

└─ Rep ─┘

119

Tension

Correct tension is vitally important, yet it is something often disregarded even by experienced knitters.

All knitting patterns are accompanied by a tension measurement. This refers to the number of stitches and rows there are to a given measurement (usually 10cm) and is the basis on which all the pattern calculations have been made. Unless this tension is matched by the knitter the garment will not be the correct size.

Tension is affected by several factors. Two of them – needle size and stitch pattern – are also specified in the tension measurement given in every pattern. The third, yarn, is assumed to be the yarn specified in the materials section of the pattern and will not be mentioned in the tension measurement unless there are several yarns or other special circumstances (such as the yarn being used double). The fourth factor, and the one most ignored, is the knitter.

STITCH PATTERN
Different stitch patterns produce different tensions, even where the needle size, yarn and knitter remain the same. This is obvious when comparing stitches like lace and rib that are totally different in character. Lace patterns are very open and loose and have fewer stitches to 10cm than ribs, which are designed to pull inwards and have more stitches to 10cm. However, it is also true of stitch patterns that are ostensibly similar like, for example, garter stitch and stocking stitch. As a result you cannot substitute a new stitch for the one given in a pattern and assume that the overall measurements will stay the same. When checking your tension for a particular pattern the stitch pattern specified in the tension measurement must be used for the tension sample.

NEEDLE SIZE
Since tension is, in effect, a measure of the size of individual stitches the size of the needles is obviously directly linked. The larger the needles the larger will be the stitches and the looser the tension – there will be fewer stitches and rows to the square centimetre. Smaller needles produce tighter tension and therefore more stitches and rows to the square centimetre.

YARN
Patterns worked in thicker yarns will have fewer stitches and rows to the square centimetre than those worked in finer yarns. It is even more important than usual to make a careful tension check when you are substituting a different yarn for the one specified or when patterns specify only generic types of yarn, as in this book.

THE KNITTER
The effect of the individual knitter on tension is often underestimated, yet it is as important as any of the other factors. It is the knitter who controls the flow of yarn through the fingers, putting more or less tension on the thread. Some people naturally knit more loosely than others. Tension is an entirely personal thing like a signature. For this reason it is not advisable for two people to work on different parts of the same garment. If they do, each knitter should check her or his tension independently of the other one. They may well need to use different needle sizes to achieve the correct pattern tension.

The tension measurement given in the pattern is the tension of the designer of the pattern and is quite likely to be different from that of the individual knitter. However, in order to complete the pattern successfully and produce a garment with the correct measurements, it is essential for the knitter to adjust her or his tension to match that of the pattern. This cannot be done by attempting to knit more tightly or more loosely than usual. It must be done by changing to a smaller or larger needle size. The needle size stated in the materials and tension section of patterns is never more than a rough guide to the size that should actually be used. It is a recommended starting point for making tension samples. In many cases it will be necessary to use a different size. In such cases, if larger or smaller needles are used for other parts of the pattern (the rib, for example) these must also be adjusted in the same direction.

MAKING A TENSION SAMPLE
In order to check your tension it is necessary to make tension samples. Using the recommended needle size and the yarn specified in the materials section of the

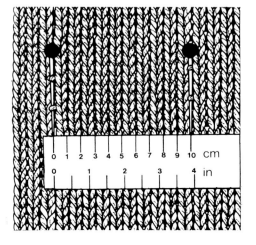

pattern (or in the tension measurement if there is more than one type of yarn), knit up a square in the stitch pattern given in the tension measurement. Cast on a few more stitches than the figure given for the stitch tension and work a few more rows than the figure given for the row tension. Cast off as usual and block and press the sample as instructed in the making up section of the pattern or on the ball band of the yarn. It may be necessary to make up several more samples using different needle sizes.

MEASURING TENSION
Place the sample on a flat surface. Take a rigid ruler and place it horizontally on the sample, lining it up along the bottom of a row of stitches. Mark the zero point with a pin on the left-hand side of a stitch. Mark the 10cm point with another pin. Count the number of stitches between the pins including half stitches if any. This will give you the figure for the stitch tension of the sample.

Now place the ruler vertically on the sample aligning it along one side of a column of stitches. Pin the zero and 10cm points. Count the number of rows between the pins to give the figure for the row tension of the sample. If there are fewer stitches and rows than those given for the pattern tension, the sample is too loose. Knit up a sample using the next smallest needle size and measure it again. If there are too many rows and stitches, the sample is too tight. Knit up a sample using the next largest size and measure it again. Carry on in this way, changing the size of the needles until the tension of the pattern is matched. Occasionally it is impossible to match both stitch and row tension. In such cases choose a needle size that will give you the correct stitch tension, working more or fewer rows to adjust the length.

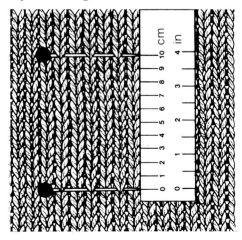

BASIC STITCHES

Most of the tension measurements in this book are given over basic stitches involving straightforward combinations of knit and purl stitches. It is assumed in the patterns that knitters know these stitches by heart. For those who do not, here is a brief refresher course on how to work them. Unless otherwise stated, the stitch patterns can be worked over any number of stitches.

Garter stitch is worked by knitting every stitch of every row, producing a fabric with marked horizontal ridges. It can also be worked by purling every stitch of every row. In circular knitting the rounds are knitted and purled alternately. To obtain a neat edge in garter stitch when it is used for borders, slip the edge stitch on every alternate row.

Stocking stitch is worked by knitting every stitch in right-side rows and purling every stitch in wrong-side rows. It produces a smooth fabric that curls inwards and is suitable for the body of a garment but not usually for the edges. In circular knitting every round is knitted.

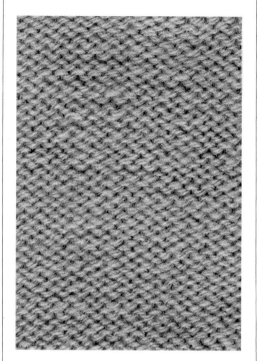

Reverse stocking stitch is worked by purling every stitch in right-side rows and knitting every stitch in wrong-side rows. In circular knitting all the rows are purled.

K1, P1 rib Sometimes called single rib, this stitch is worked by knitting and purling stitches alternately in the first row. In every subsequent row the stitches that were knitted the previous row are purled and the stitches that were purled are knitted. In circular knitting the same stitches are purled or knitted in every round. In flat knitting K1, P1 rib can be worked over an odd or even number of stitches. In circular knitting it can only be worked over an even number of stitches.

K2, P2 rib Sometimes called double rib, this stitch is worked by knitting and purling pairs of stitches alternately in the first row. In every subsequent row knit the stitches that were purled the previous row and purl the stitches that were knitted. In circular knitting the same stitches are knitted or purled in every round. In flat knitting K2, P2 rib must be worked over an even number of stitches. In circular knitting it must be worked over a multiple of four stitches.

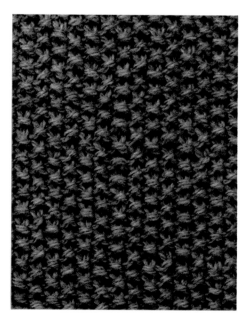

Moss stitch is suitable for the body of a garment and for borders. It is worked by knitting and purling stitches alternately in the first row. In all subsequent rows the stitches that were knitted the previous row are again knitted and the stitches that were purled are again purled. In circular knitting the stitches that were knitted the previous row are purled and the stitches that were purled are knitted. In flat knitting moss stitch can be worked over any number of stitches. In circular knitting it must be worked over an even number of stitches.

Making Up
Extra care in making up will give a garment a professional finish.

That depressing 'homemade' look so common in handknits is often the result of careless making up. Many knitters devote endless time and patience to their knitting but rush the making up process in their eagerness to be finished. Time spent at this stage means that all the labours of the previous days, weeks or even months will not be wasted. The making up section of a pattern tells you how to seam the various pieces together and in what order. But before you even begin to join seams there are several important processes to go through that most patterns do not bother to mention.

ENDS
During the course of the knitting it will have been necessary to join in a new ball of yarn several times. Unless the yarn ends have been spliced together there will be many long loose ends which have to be darned in. These should be at the edges of each piece since it is usual to join in a new ball of yarn at the beginning of a row rather than in the middle. Darn in each end separately up the sides of the knitting or along edges that will be seamed. Try to avoid darning ends into the centre as this can show on the right side. Do not simply knot the ends and cut them off as they can work loose during wear. Darn in at least 5cm of every end. Trim off the remainder.

BLOCKING
All the component pieces of the garment must be pinned out to the correct shape and measurements before seaming. This process is called blocking. Fold a white towel or blanket to make a smooth pad and place it on a flat hard surface. Place the garment pieces wrong side up on the pad and pin it out all round, checking the measurements of each part against the measurement diagram as you do so. Slight discrepancies in the measurements can often be adjusted by stretching or easing the knitting just a little. Make sure that edges that should be straight are pinned out straight and that curves and other

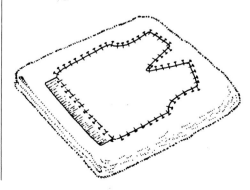

shaped edges are smooth. Push the pins into the pad right up to the head, spacing them a few centimetres apart. Do not pin around ribbed edges. These should be allowed to pull in naturally. Pin along the join between the ribbed sections and the rest of the garment.

PRESSING
Check the pressing instructions on the ball band of the yarn. The symbols below are the relevant ones. Many yarns, especially synthetics, should not be pressed at all as they will suffer heat damage or the finish will be adversely affected. Garments worked in such yarns can be sprayed lightly with water and allowed to dry into shape. If the yarn can be pressed, cover the blocked garment with a clean white cloth – damp for wool, dry for synthetics and mixtures. Using the appropriate heat setting, press the knitting using up and down rather than sliding movements. Very few garments benefit from heavy pressing so use a light touch and do not hold the iron on the garment for any length of time. Do not press garter stitch or ribbing or heavily textured patterns like bobbles and cables. Leave the knitting to dry naturally before removing the pins.

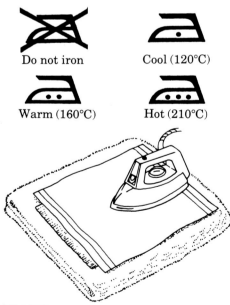

Do not iron   Cool (120°C)

Warm (160°C)   Hot (210°C)

SEAMS
Work the seams in the order given in the making up section of the pattern. There is usually a good reason for it. There may, for example, be a neckband to work. This will necessitate first joining one of the shoulder seams so that it can be worked in one piece and it is easier to do this before the side seams have been joined. Some

knitters prefer to work neckbands in the round so that there is no join. In this case, both shoulder seams should be joined first.

If possible join seams with the same yarn as that used for the knitting. If the yarn is very thick or textured use a finer smooth yarn in the same colour. When working any seam take care not to split the knitted stitches. Use a round-ended wool needle and insert it between or through the centre of stitches rather than through the yarn itself.

The choice of seam is generally left up to the knitter. There are several that are suitable for joining knitted garments. *Backstitch* seams are very strong but can be bulky. Use them for shoulder seams and for setting in sleeves. Work the seam one stitch from the edge from right to left.

Flat seams are used to join on borders such as buttonbands and buttonhole bands that have been made separately and where the join is likely to be visible.

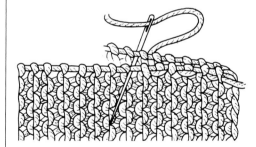

Invisible seams are ideal for joining the side seams of garments made in stocking stitch. They are worked with the right side facing and from the bottom of the seam to the top.

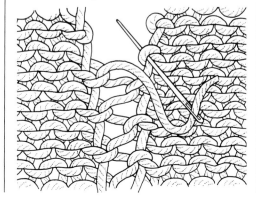

GRAFTING

Grafting produces a completely invisible join but it can only be used on straight horizontal edges with an equal number of stitches in each edge. If a join is to be grafted do not cast off the stitches on each edge. Place one set of stitches on a spare needle with the point on the right and the other on a spare needle with the point on the left. Now position the needles so that both are pointing to the right and the stitches are opposite each other. Thread a wool needle with matching yarn and graft the two sets of stitches together as shown. The grafting thread in the diagram is in a contrast colour to make it clearer. As each stitch is secured with the grafting thread withdraw the needle from it. Take care to match the original tension as closely as possible.

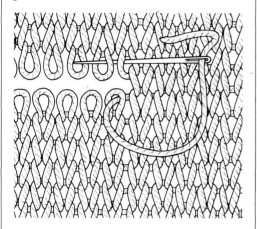

SWISS DARNING

The making up stage is the time when any additional embroidery, beading or other decoration is worked on the garment. Any of the more conventional embroidery stitches can be used on knitwear but there is also a stitch which is special to it. Swiss darning imitates the form of stocking stitch. Worked in matching yarn it is a useful reinforcing technique. Worked in contrast colours it enables you to work colour patterns and motifs on knitwear that look as if they have been knitted in. The Swiss darning stitches must cover the knitted background stitches completely if they are to be fully effective so use a yarn that is the same weight and thickness as the original one.

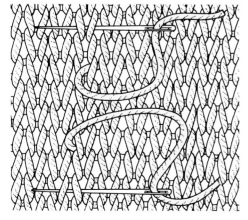

SETTING IN SLEEVES

There are four main sleeve types common in knitted garments: raglan, set-in, flat and French. They are all made up in slightly different ways though the pattern may only say, 'Set in sleeves.'

Raglan seams are joined before the side seams. Sometimes three of the seams are joined first leaving one of the back ones open, then a neckband is knitted and the fourth seam joined. The underarm and side seams are joined in one.

Set-in sleeves are usually made up separately and then joined to the body of the garment. Join the shoulder and side seams, then join the underarm seam. With the sleeve turned right side out and the body wrong side out fit the sleeve in position matching the underarm seam with the side seam and the sleeve head with the shoulder seam. Pin round the armhole easing in any fullness round the sleeve head. Join the armhole seam with a backstitch seam.

Flat sleeves have no shaping on the sleeve head, nor is there shaping on the body. Join the shoulder seams. Place the centre of the cast-off edge of the sleeve to the shoulder seam. Join the armhole seam, then the side and underarm seams in one.

French sleeves have no shaping on the sleeve head and there is only simple cast-off shaping on the body. Join the shoulder seam. Place the centre of the cast-off edge of the sleeve to the shoulder seam and join the straight part of the armhole seam. Now join the cast-off stitches at the underarm to the last few rows of the sleeve.

POCKETS

The nature of the making up process for pockets depends on whether it is a patch pocket, or a pocket that is set in horizontally, vertically or into the side seams. If a pattern does not include instructions for a pocket it is very easy to make a patch or side seam pocket after the rest of the garment is finished.

Patch pockets can be made either in the same yarn and stitch pattern as the main part of the garment or in a contrast. Often they are square or rectangular but they can be any shape. The edging of the pocket opening is made at the same time as the rest of the pocket. It should be in a suitable border stitch like rib, moss stitch or garter stitch. Sew the pocket on during the making up stage either decoratively with bold embroidery stitches or invisibly, using either neat slipstitching or, for a very firm and totally invisible join, in Swiss darning through both thicknesses in a matching yarn. This latter join only works if the pocket and background are in stocking stitch.

Horizontal pockets are knitted into the garment during the course of the work. The pocket lining may also be knitted in or it can be worked separately and sewn in afterwards. During the making up stage it is usually necessary to attach the pocket lining to the inside of the garment using neat slipstitching in a matching yarn, and to work a pocket edging. Slipstitch the row ends of the pocket edging to the right side of the garment.

Vertical pockets are also knitted in as you go along and the lining either made separately or knitted in. When slipstitching the lining to the inside of the garment make sure it is aligned with the first and last rows of the pocket opening to avoid puckering on the right side.

Side seam pockets are common on jackets and cardigans. The lining is made separately in the form of a rectangular bag and the opening of the bag is stitched into the seam, half to the back of the garment and half to the front. Often there is no edging, and the opening is closed with buttons and button loops or a zip.

BUTTONS

Choose buttons that are slightly bigger than the actual measurement of the buttonhole and make sure they are not too heavy for the fabric. Sew them on with the yarn used for the garment or, if it is too bulky, in a finer matching yarn. The edges of the buttonhole can, if required, be reinforced by working buttonhole stitch round the edges as in dressmaking.

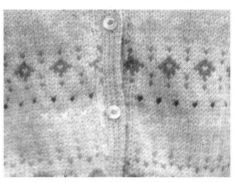

ZIPS

Zips are often used to close front openings of jackets or cardigans and for pocket tops. The required length is usually specified in the materials. If the length of the garment has been altered, remember to buy a different length zip. It should be slightly shorter rather than longer than the actual length of the opening. Insert the zip closed, making sure that both sides of the opening match and that the edges of the knitting do not overlap the zip teeth. Pin it in position, stretching it slightly if necessary (never stretch the knitting to fit the zip). Fold in the extra tape at the top of the opening and stitch the zip in place using a backstitch seam.

Aftercare

The life of knitted garments can be prolonged by giving special attention to washing and cleaning.

Hand knitting is a pleasurable but time-consuming craft and the materials involved are relatively expensive so it makes a good deal of sense to look after your garments really well. Whatever the yarn used all knitwear requires very careful washing and cleaning. Even those yarns marked 'easy-care' and 'machine washable' benefit from more gentle handling from time to time. In order to choose the correct cleaning method it is essential to know the fibre composition of the yarn. The ball band should contain this information and it may also display the symbols of the International Textile Care Labelling Code, of which the relevant ones are reproduced here.

DRY-CLEANING
Many yarns, including wool, can be dry-cleaned and this can be a very practical solution where time is short. However, repeated dry-cleaning eventually removes the softness of the yarn and the elasticity of ribbing so it is advisable to wash such garments occasionally to restore these properties. Some synthetic yarns and mixtures need special care during dry-cleaning. Check the ball band and make sure the dry-cleaner has all the relevant information.

WASHING
Unless the ball band contains specific information to the contrary all knitwear should be hand-washed. It is also safest to hand-wash any garment where the fibre content of the yarn is unknown. Careless washing, either by machine or by hand, causes the fibres of the yarn to mat together or 'felt'. This is particularly true of yarns made from pure animal fibres like wool, alpaca and mohair. There is no remedy for felting but it can be considerably delayed and often prevented indefinitely by careful, gentle hand-washing.

Friction is one of the many causes of felting so wash knitwear frequently to avoid the necessity of rubbing to remove ingrained dirt. Use a detergent specially made for wool or soap flakes, adding only the recommended amount to the washing water. Make sure the bowl is large enough to take the garment comfortably and wash only one garment at a time. Half fill the bowl with hot water and dissolve the detergent completely. Add enough cold water to make the water hand-hot and to cover the garment completely. The actual washing process should take as short a time as possible. Never leave knitwear to soak. Squeeze the garment gently in the warm suds to release the dirt. Turn it over, supporting the weight with both hands.

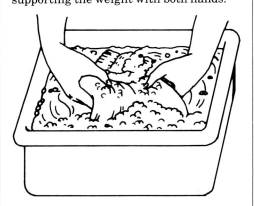

RINSING
Use plenty of water for rinsing, applying the same gentleness of touch as to the washing process. The rinsing water should be the same temperature as the washing water and there should be plenty of room for the garment to circulate freely. To make sure every trace of soap has been completely removed, rinse the garment several times in fresh water. Fabric conditioner can be added to the last rinse if required. Squeeze the excess water out of the garment. Do not wring it.

DRYING
Roll the garment up in a thick clean towel to remove as much of the remaining water as possible. Alternatively, spin it briefly if

	MACHINE	HAND WASH
4/50	Hand-hot medium wash	Hand-hot
	Cold rinse. Short spin or drip dry	

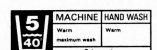

Nylon; polyester; cotton and viscose articles with special finishes; acrylic/cotton mixtures; coloured polyester/cotton mixtures.

	MACHINE	HAND WASH
5/40	Warm maximum wash	Warm
	Spin or wring	

Cotton, linen or viscose articles where colours are fast at 40°C, but not at 60°C.

	MACHINE	HAND WASH
6/40	Warm minimum wash	Warm
	Cold rinse. Short spin. Do not wring	

Acrylics; acetate and triacetate, including mixtures with wool; polyester/wool blends.

	MACHINE	HAND WASH
7/40	Warm minimum wash	Warm Do not rub
	Spin. Do not hand wring	

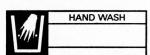

Wool, wool mixtures with cotton or viscose; silk.

	HAND WASH

Articles which must not be machine washed.

Do not wash.

Chlorine bleach may be used.

Chlorine bleach may not be used.

 (A) Dry cleanable in all solvents.

 (P) Dry cleanable in perchloroethylene, white spirit, Solvent 113 and Solvent 11.

 (P) May be cleaned with the same solvents shown for ℗ but with a strict limitation on the addition of water during cleaning and/or certain restrictions concerning mechanical action or drying temperature or both.

 (F) Dry cleanable in white spirit and Solvent 113.

 (F) May be cleaned with the same solvents shown for Ⓕ but with a strict limitation on the addition of water during cleaning and/or certain restrictions concerning mechanical action or drying temperature or both.

 Do not dry clean.

 Tumble drying beneficial.

 Do not tumble dry.

a drier is available. Do not use a tumble drier especially if the yarn contains synthetic fibres subject to heat damage. Complete the drying process with the garment laid flat and eased into shape on a dry towel, away from sunlight or any direct source of heat. Leave it until it is completely dry. Store knitwear in a clean dry drawer rather than on hangers. Protect natural fibres with mothballs.

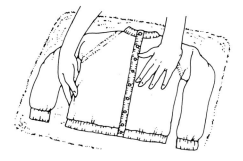

PILLING
After a while some garments become affected by 'pilling', where small balls of loose fibres form on the surface of the fabric. This effect can be minimised by washing garments inside out. To remove the pills, either pull them off or cut them off with a razor blade or sharp scissors.

SNAGGING
It's almost impossible not to snag knitwear at sometime or other. Sometimes a whole row of stitches can be tightened up in this way. Using the point of a knitting needle and beginning at the snag, gradually ease the stitches back to the correct size. Push any remaining slack to the back of the work. Cut the loop and darn in the loose ends.

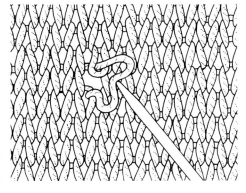

REPAIRING KNITWEAR
Some predictable repairs can be prevented during the making of a garment. Ribbed edges, for example, are subject to a great deal of wear and tear. To strengthen the edge cast it on or off using a double thickness of yarn. Some parts of a garment, elbows, for example, often wear thin after a while. These can be reinforced by working Swiss darning over them, using a matching yarn.

Small holes can be repaired by rebuilding the stitches either by grafting, if only one row is affected, or by darning as shown. Large holes can be patched, either with knitted patches or, if it can be done decoratively, with patches made of leather or fabric.

Where the damage is extensive it may be necessary to reknit whole sections of the garment. Ribbed neckbands can easily be unravelled back to the main body of the

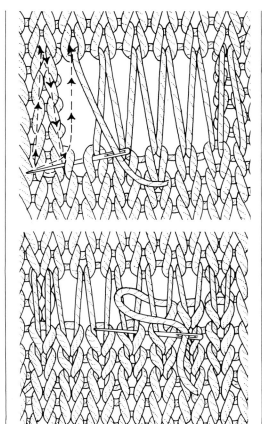

garment. Reknit them either in the same or a contrast colour. It is also possible to reknit ribbed edges where they form the cast-on edge of the garment as is often the case on sleeves and sweater fronts and backs. Unpick the relevant seams, either the sleeve seam or the sides seams, and pull a thread just above the point where the rib ends. Cut the yarn and, using a knitting needle, ease the stitches apart all along that row, removing the original yarn as you go. Pick up the stitches along the upper edge of the gap and reknit the rib downwards, following the original instructions but decreasing rather than increasing and *vice versa*.

ALTERATIONS
While it is quite impractical to alter the width of knitted garments, alterations to the length are relatively easy. Simply pull a thread as given above, pick up the stitches on either side of the gap and add as many rows as required. Finally graft the stitches on each side of the gap together. To shorten a garment, unravel as many rows as required before grafting the two sets of stitches together. Any added length can be worked either in the original yarn, if there is any left, or in one or more contrast colours. Make sure the stripes are at the same level on the back and front.

ADAPTING KNITWEAR
By combining the techniques for repairing and altering knitwear it is possible to give a well-worn garment a new lease of life with some simple adaptations. A plain round-necked sweater can be striped and given contrasting welts, for example. Make it into a slipover by removing the sleeves and adding armbands. Any garment knitted in stocking stitch can be brightened up with some Swiss-darned motifs or patterns. Change the shape of a

collar or the length of a sleeve. Shorten a dress into a sweater or a coat into a cardigan. When remodelling knitwear it is even possible to cut the fabric if you work two rows of machine stitching on each side of the proposed cut to secure the stitches.

RECYCLING YARN
Clothes which are quite literally beyond repair, alteration or adaptation can, in some circumstances, be recycled. One of the advantages of hand-knitting is that the yarn from unsuccessful or discarded garments can often be unravelled, reconstituted virtually in its original form and re-used for something else. The effectiveness of this operation depends largely on the type of yarn, how long it has been knitted up and how well it has been cared for during that time. Heavily felted garments cannot be unravelled. Throw them away or use them for rag rugs. It is also difficult to unravel textured yarns like bouclé or hairy ones like mohair and angora. Cotton yarns tend to become unattractively stringy when unravelled as do many synthetics. The best chances of success are provided by plain good-quality woollen yarns. These can be unravelled in reasonably good condition several years after they were originally knitted up.

Having decided that the garment in question is a suitable candidate for recycling, unpick all the seams in reverse order to the original making up. Resist the temptation to cut seams or you will be left with lots of short lengths. When the garment has been dismantled, taking each section in turn, loosen the last stitch in the cast-off edge and thread the end of the yarn through it. Pull on the end to unravel the yarn. Wind it into loose hanks as you unravel. Tie the hanks in several places to prevent tangling. Inevitably, the yarn will be crinkly and it must be straightened before it can be reknitted. Either steam the yarn gently in the steam from a boiling kettle or wash it and dry it as described earlier for garments. When the yarn is completely dry, rewind it in balls ready for reknitting.

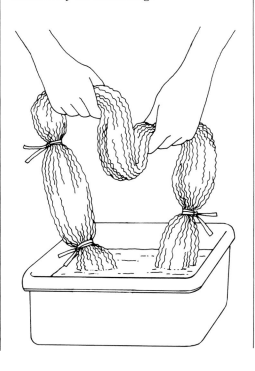

Original Yarns

ORIGINAL YARNS

For those who are able to obtain them, the following list describes the yarns originally used to knit up the garments on pages 8–111. Most of them are from French spinners or shops whose yarns are available in the UK and the USA only on a limited basis. The addresses of the appropriate agents, where they exist, are also given and readers may write to them for lists of stockists.

page 8
Véra Finbert Coton Zabeth

page 10
Marigold 4 fils

page 12
(350)400(450)g Phildar Lugano and 200g Phildar Sunset (used together)

page 14
Anny Blatt No 4

page 16
Huguet Laine de pays 3 fils (used double)

page 18
Marigold 4 fils

page 20
Pingouin Super 4

page 22
Phildar Midship (used double)

page 24
Berger du Nord Classique

page 26
Phildar Shoot

page 28
Boisson Lin assoupli (used double)

page 30
Georges Picaud Coton rustique (four strands used together)

page 32
Georges Picaud Laine et coton

page 34
Georges Picaud Coton tweed

page 36
Anny Blatt Lord' Anny

page 38
Huguet Coton Epsom

page 40
Filatures de Paris Coton louisiane

page 42
Charier Coton mat

page 44
La Droguerie Coton fin (A) and La Droguerie Étincelle (B, used double)

page 46
La Droguerie Coton fin No 7 (3 strands used together)

page 48
Anny Blatt Kid Anny

page 50
Welcomme Pernelle Touareg

page 52
Berger du Nord Island light

page 54
Plassard Harmonieuse

page 56
Bouton d'Or Frigolo

page 58
Sofil Sonate

page 60
Berger du Nord Laine d'Islande

page 62
Berger du Nord Prodiges

page 64
Sofil Alpaga

page 66
Jean Roulotte Cachemire

page 68
Chanteleine Marly Courtelle

page 70
Pingouin Type Shetland

page 72
Filatures de Paris Fleur de laine

page 74
Marigold 3 fils

page 76
Georges Picaud Feu vert

page 78
Sofil Sofiluge

page 80
(800)850(900)g Houard Laine ecru and (150)200(250)g Bischwiller Boucryl (used together)

page 82
Georges Picaud Sport

page 84
Bouton d'Or Super vaporeux

page 86
Georges Picaud Sport

page 88
Georges Picaud Sport

page 90
Huguet Laine de pays 5 fils

page 92
Anny Blatt Angora

page 94
Frizelle Tweed Actuel Courtelle

page 96
Chat Botté No 6

page 98
Berger du Nord Laine d'Islande

page 100
Chat Botté Perlé fine (used double)

page 102
Rouet d'Argent Laine rustique 3 fils

page 104
Pingouin Super 4

page 107
Anny Blatt Zealand

ADDRESSES

Anny Blatt
1–3 Mortimer Street
London W1
UK

Anny Blatt
24770 Crestview Court
Farmington
MI 01887
USA

Berger du Nord
Brookman & Sons Inc
4872 NE 12th Avenue
Fort Lauderdale
FL 33334
USA

Chanteleine
Textile Artists Supply
3006 San Pablo Avenue
Berkeley
CA 94702
USA

Chat Botté
Grove of Thame
Lupton Road Industrial Estate
Thame
Oxfordshire OX9 3RR
UK

Phildar (UK) Ltd
4 Gambrel Road
Westgate Industrial Estate
Northampton
UK

Phildar Inc
6438 Dawson Boulevard
Norcross
GA 30093
USA

Georges Picaud
Priory Yarns
48 Station Road
Ossett
Wakefield
Yorkshire
UK

Georges Picaud
Merino Yarn Co
230 Fifth Avenue
New York
NY 10001
USA

Pingouin
French Wools
7–11 Lexington Street
London W1
UK

Pingouin
PO Box 100
Highway 45
Jamestown
SC 29453
USA